AF426644

Far From The Twisted Reach

The Last Road Trip Ever

Matt Bindig

ISBN: 978-1-953610-46-1
         979-8-218-23763-9

1. Nonfiction>Memoir
2. Autobiographical
3. Nonfiction> Travelogue> United States
4. Memoir>Family Life
5. Relationships

Cover design by Diane and Anna Bond.
All photos, including the cover, were taken by the author.

NFB
<<<>>>
NFB Publishing/Amelia Press
119 Dorchester Road
Buffalo, New York 14213

For more information visit
Nfbpublishing.com

*For my wife and children.
May it last through the night.*

ALSO BY MATT BINDIG

Nothing Here Is Real

This book is a memoir centered on events that took place
in the summer of 2019. It is rooted in story-truth. Though
the hard details here are surely fact, specific conversations
and the like are translated through the filter of memory.

And take me disappearing
Through the smoke rings of my mind
Down the foggy ruins of time
Far past the frozen leaves
The haunted frightened trees
Out to the windy beach
Far from the twisted reach of crazy sorrow

— *Mr. Tambourine Man*. Bob Dylan.

3.13.23

Dear Reader,

I sat down to begin this project with three reminders scribbled on a sticky note attached to the side of my computer screen. Be honest. Write the type of story you want to read. Say it any damn way you please. And I stuck to each one of them.

I've done my best to tell this story in a way that reflects my frame of mind at the time we took our trip — even if doing so sometimes makes me cringe with embarrassment now. So much has changed since I first started writing this book, both within and without, but there's no eraser big enough to alter the past, and memory is a fickle muse. Some things I say here, and the way I say them, might hurt your feelings — but that's the way it is.

I've chosen to let these moments stand as a little gift to all of you. It might just be that, like me, you sometimes lose sight of nuances and the sensibilities you hold dear when faced with a wolf scratching at your door. And, like so many other people I know who are struggling, that is where I was at the beginning of this journey — holding my shoulder against the splintering wood as the raging beast of madness snapped at me, doing its best to get inside my head, from just outside the threshold.

No one is perfect. It's my take that the world would be a whole lot better off if we collectively recognized that and handed out our grace accordingly. At the very least, we can start by listening to one another.

Either way, I want you to *feel* the Truth. Mine. Yours. Ours. That's what I'm after.

No hard feelings.

Matt Bindig

Table of Contents

To The Woods
(Prologue)

I SOMETIMES THINK OF adult life as a table full of empty drinking glasses. You stand in front of it, with a pitcher full of water in your hands, and it's your job to fill the glasses up. The glasses are all the things in your life that make your life, *your life*: your spouse, your kids, your health, your job, your faith, your finances, your house, your lawn, your dog, your social life, your community engagement, the sports teams you follow, your reading list, the things you do "just for fun" . . . you get the idea.

The water in the pitcher represents your energy and objective time. Some people have more glasses on the table than others, but there are always just twenty-four hours in a day, regardless of how much you have to or want to get done. So now you've got some decisions to make. Do you fill the most important ones up all the way and let the others sit dry? Or do you fill all of them up just a little bit, trying your best to even things out? Maybe you fill up some of the main ones mostly to the top and then splash a little water in the remaining glasses, just so they don't feel neglected. After all, equal and *fair* are not always the same thing.

Any way you look at it, the way you decide to fill up your glasses is basically who you are. You might think you're a really good Dad, but if your Golf Glass is overflowing and your Dad Glass isn't even half full, the chances are you're not what you say you are. It's just the truth.

Now to some degree, you can affect the level of water in your pitcher: get enough sleep, eat right, have regular sex, make sure to exercise — basically take care of yourself and spend more time doing meaningful things that bring you joy and less time with the have-tos that just suck, and the water level in your pitcher will probably go up. This is no secret: when you feel good (physically, mentally, spiritually) you've got more energy to do more things, which in turn keeps you feeling good so you'll have more energy to do more things. But here's the great rub: each of those energy-giving, water-raising things is also a glass begging for attention. You've got to fill them up right if you want them to work properly for you, which is far easier said than done.

Let me show you what I mean.

Let's say each night, you get to bed by 9:00 p.m. so you'll be sure to get a good eight hours of sleep. That way, you won't be tired and grumpy (and therefore less likely to actually get up) when your alarm goes off at 5:00 a.m., which is when you have to set it if you want to get a tough workout in, shower, dress, and eat a good breakfast before jumping in the car and driving to work without being stressed about time (who needs to start their day stressed?).

Everything is great so far. You're at work, well rested, with a morning workout under your belt. Now let's say, just for the sake of argument, that work goes relatively smoothly, no major blow-ups or miscues, no interpersonal drama or clumsy communication that you have to follow-up on later in the day. You do your job well. Great day; just a handful of papers you have to take home to look over and a few emails to send out before tomorrow.

On the way home, you go out of your way to stop at the local co-op to pick up some farm-fresh grub for dinner. Your wife's been on you about the chips and beer, so you want to show her that you've been listening; you're making an effort. In fact you spent your lunch hour looking up the ingredients you'll need for dinner. The co-op is a little out of the way and costs more than the regular grocery store, but good food is good fuel. It's worth it.

You get home, walk the dog (because having a dog gives you joy), make a savory meal, chat with your wife, clean up the dishes, and sit down to finish up those papers and emails you need to have done by tomorrow.

Your day has been pretty great so far, so you've still got lots of water in your pitcher. By the time you get your work done, scan the news, and answer a few personal texts it's 8:00 p.m.. The news is annoying. I mean, really maddening actually, but you try your best to put it out of mind as you take a quick shower so you won't stink when it's time for sex.

When you get out of the shower, you find that your wife hasn't finished her take-home work yet. Plus she's actually had a really shitty day and she really wants to talk about it. You already talked about it for most of dinner but, no matter. Turns out the tech guy, who's a creepy jerk anyway, couldn't figure out the glitch that's preventing her from finishing up the project she started yesterday. That threw everything off, which is why it's after eight at night now and she's still working. Plus, her friend called last night crying about some problem her kid was having in school. Your wife insists that she really ought to call her friend back.

Like a good husband, you talk this all through (maybe over a glass of wine), but now it's 8:45 and the wine is making you a little sleepy. No, not sleepy, *tired* (I mean, Jesus, you did get up at 5:00 *a.m.* to work out). So you go upstairs to bed to read a little while your wife makes that "quick call" — it's never a quick call — to her friend, but you're not happy about it. I mean time's a wasting here.

By the time she gets off the phone with her friend and does all of her "self-care" with those twenty-some bottles of cream and shit she keeps in the bathroom, it'll be 9:20. At this rate, if you have sex, even quick meaningless sex with no foreplay what-so-ever, you'll already be running late on your fucking Zen fill-the-right-glasses-up schedule. Now, the only way you'll get those eight hours is if you set your alarm for later, but that'll mean cutting back on your workout. And even as you think all of this, another part of your brain will be like, "My God, when did sex become so transactional? I mean remember that time in college . . . it wasn't like this back then. But now I'm tired and I've got to get up. I might as well jerk off if this is what it's going to be like. But then how pathetic is that?"

So, when your wife gets into bed, *at 9:25*, you can't hide your resentment and instead of rubbing her back and being all romantic and shit, you pick a fight about your sex life and how it needs to be a priority. The next thing you know it's 10:07, and even though you've stopped arguing, there's *no way* you're having sex, even bad, make-up sex because now you're really tired and there's no fucking chance you're going to want to pop out of bed come 5:00 a.m. tomorrow to work out.

See what I mean?

And this is when you're feeling good. I mean actually, consciously trying. Imagine a bad day. And I haven't even mentioned what happens when you add three kids, and jobs (that's jobs *plural*), a "charming" 100 year old house, a couple of volunteer coaching gigs, and a stint as a sometimes Sunday School teacher to the mix.

Lots of glasses begging for water and your pitcher has a leak.

THE first time Theresa and I sat down to formally talk about our Western Adventure was in January 2019. I say "formally" talk because we had mentioned the idea of a big trip plenty, but we never seemed able to find the right amount of time to really dig into talking about the idea much less actually planning it. Every time it seemed like we'd be able to sit down and really talk about it, something else "more pressing" would come up and we'd have to settle to agree to talk about it at some point . . . later. When you're a parent, it's always later.

So when I finally managed to get Theresa out of the house with a glass of wine in front of her, and her undivided attention focused on the task at hand, I was determined to make the most of the moment.

I had maps with *Indiana Jones* lines indicating our potential path drawn on them, a dated and detailed itinerary, even some tour books I'd picked up at the local AAA.

The Plan, as I pitched it, was to leave on June 27th, the day after school let out for the summer, and come back on August 25th, two days before I had to return to work the next year. Over those almost ten weeks, we'd take Route Twenty across the Northern states. Once we hit the West coast, we'd turn down Route One all along the Pacific. Once we hit San Diego, we'd snake our way back home across the South, cutting up North again at a diagonal once we passed through Texas.

When I was finished, I leaned over the map and took her hand. "What do you think?"

"Wow, that's a lot of time in the car. I mean that's a lot of driving. Would it be our car?"

"Yeah, the van."

"That's just, you know, a lot of miles."

"The van's in good shape."

"Maybe we could rent a van; put all that wear and tear on somebody else's car. Or a motorhome. A motorhome would be fun. Remember my family had one when I was a kid. We'd drive down to Virginia to visit my Aunt Gertrude . . ."

"I know all about the motorhome, Theresa. It was rotting in your parents' driveway when we first started dating, remember?"

"It was old then, but when my sister and I were little . . ."

"Look, I'm not driving a rented motorhome across the country, okay. Simple pictures are best," I said, quoting the title of one of our kids' favorite books from when they were really little. "Let's just take our car."

"Okay, but how much do you think all this will cost? I mean, with all that time away. I won't be able to work, and we'll have to stay in a lot of hotels."

"No, we'll camp out. We've got a great tent."

"You want to camp for ten weeks?"

"Yes."

"Harper is seven."

"Okay, so we'll camp *most* nights and stay in a hotel or something every third night. Break it up like that."

"Okay, what about the dog? We'll have to board Rosie then, right?"

"No, we'll bring her with us. She does great in the crate, so the ride won't be a problem. She's a great dog. She'll love the adventure."

"Not all campgrounds let dogs stay and most hotels don't. And think about space. All five of us in the van, *plus* the dog and our stuff."

"So we'll only stay in campgrounds that let you have dogs. I'll do all the research and find the hotels that let dogs stay. Listen, we'll put most of our stuff on the roof. That's why we have a luggage rack. It'll work out, okay?" I finished the last of my whiskey and tried to look her straight in the eyes, but she was shaking her head and looking over at a couple at the next table.

"Theresa, we can make excuses about this our whole lives. It's like with having kids, right? There's never a perfect time. There's never enough money. There are always things to figure out. But we got this. We can do it. I just don't want it to be like The Trail, you know? We were reasonable about that, pushed it off until later, and now, I just can't see us ever doing that. Can you? I don't want that to happen with this trip."

"The Trail was different. That was just us."

WHEN I first started teaching at Williston, a woman in the math department, Ann Vandenberg, had just returned from hiking The Appalachian Trail. She spoke about her trip at a school assembly, and when I asked to hear more, we set up regular coffee dates to talk about what it was like to solo-hike up the east coast of the United States, from Georgia to Maine. Ann had the look of an old hippy — long, straight hair, basset hound eyes — but there was a deep spiritual sense of purpose about her, and she spoke of The Trail in those terms. Spirit. Purpose. Journey. When I left Williston to go to Harvard for graduate school, Ann gave me a small pot with three jade plants in it.

"What you give your love to will grow to fit your heart," she said.

The author — sandwiched between a pair of redwoods. Prairie Creek Redwoods State Park.

AFTER graduate school, I found a teaching job at Framingham High School, outside of Boston. Two weeks into the school year, and a month to the day after Theresa and I got married, The Twin Towers fell in New York, and the country turned upside down.

Theresa still had two years of graduate school to go, but even as I worked at a local farm stand on top of teaching and coaching (just to make ends meet), I began reading everything I could get my hands on about hiking The Appalachian Trail. Having run a marathon together the previous January, we were both in pretty good shape. Still, we took long walks every day when she got home from school, and hiked through local parks whenever we could find time on the weekends. We even took a trip up to New Hampshire to hike the portion of the trail that runs through Dartmouth's campus.

The plan was, when Theresa finished school, I'd either quit my job or take a leave of absence. Then we'd take the next six months to hike The Trail together.

It never happened.

By the time Theresa was done with graduate school, I was tired of working at Framingham. It's expensive to rent in the Boston area, and teaching at a huge and diverse public school was about as different from teaching at a prep school as you can imagine. Theresa didn't have a job lined up and, even though her oldest sister, Cathy lived in Quincy, Theresa was feeling far away from home in Upstate New York. In the spring, I started looking for jobs in the central New York area and was hired in early May to teach outside of Syracuse starting the next fall. With Theresa's graduation, our needing to move out of Massachusetts and find a new place to live in an area neither of us knew very well, and my starting a new job at yet another school, the dream of hiking The Trail just kind of got . . . lost.

"Once we get settled," we said.

Two years later, after we lost our first baby, we took a trip down through North Carolina and into Tennessee. We hiked a long section of The Trail near Clingmans Dome (the highest point of elevation on The Trail), but that was the last time we were on it.

We had Henry in 2006, Max in 2009, and Harper in 2012. It's tough to hike up the coast of America with little kids. For a while we talked about maybe, when the kids were older, pulling them out of school some spring and making the trek as a family. It's been done. But the more we got involved in our life, the more that kind of adventure just seemed impossible.

We don't talk about doing it anymore.

"But, what about the kids' sports?" Theresa said. "We've already signed them up." She started counting on her fingers. "Harper's got lacrosse, Max and Henry are both doing basketball, and Henry's got soccer on top of that. I just don't want them to miss out or get behind."

"I thought you wanted to do this," I snapped.

"I do, it's just . . ."

"Then why is everything out of your mouth a reason not to? Everything you've said amounts to 'no.'" I pushed myself away from the table as eyes around the inn turned toward my sudden movement. "I'm getting another drink."

I went to the bar and ordered two whiskeys, then stood drinking the first and pretending to care about the hockey game on TV. When I turned to go back to the table, I saw Theresa talking avidly to a man I quickly recognized as Mr. Davis, the father of one of my best friends from high school.

By the time I arrived, Mr. Davis had pulled on his glasses and was pointing to spots on the various maps splayed out across our table.

"Oh hey, Matt. Theresa was just telling me about the trip."

"Yeah, we're trying to figure it out."

"Lots of driving it sounds like."

"That's the idea," I said and took another drink. "Did you and Mrs. Davis ever take any trips like this?" I asked.

I asked partly to see if I could count on him as an ally in my quest to convince Theresa to go, and partially because I deeply admire the guy. This is the man who made me mixtapes of Led Zeppelin when I was in high school and still insisted that Grunge Rock was the best music ever made. Though he owned his own company in Buffalo and was a Clarkson graduate who wasn't above pushing the kids who hung out at his house to think through the issues of the day, he also used to hang out with his daughter and all of our friends by bonfires in the backyard, telling stories and laughing at our jokes. Rumor had it he had a "special" garden somewhere near his property.

I also knew that the Davis family regularly took exciting outdoor adventure trips. Skiing. Camping. Canoeing. You name it. The fact that he was standing there looking at my maps and my crude, naive itinerary was actually something like a blessing. I couldn't have expected better advice if I had gone to a travel agent.

"There's a lot of dead space in the middle of the country," he said. "You and I probably wouldn't mind driving for hours and hours with nothing but the horizon in front of us, Matt, but we did something like this once with the kids and it was just, a lot. A lot of driving."

"I'm thinking that's kind of the point," I stubbornly said. "The journey, not the destination, you know."

"Well, okay, but what if all your kids remember about the trip is sitting in a cramped car for hours and looking at wheat? That's a miserable journey."

"So what's your advice?" I asked.

"Why not fly out? Cut down on the drive time. Rent a car when you get out there. There's tons of space out there anyway. Don't worry, if it's driving you're after, there'll be plenty of driving to do. You've got to figure out what you really want to see and then get there and go see it."

"That's good advice," Theresa said. The bastard was a double agent.

"Let me buy you a drink." I said.

"No, I've got to go catch up with Dawn, Mrs. Davis, you know. Thanks anyways," he laughed. "Next time."

I tucked all of my maps and papers back into my folder and leaned over the table. "What do you think?" I said to Theresa.

"Well, let's say we fly out to Sarah's," Theresa's sister Sarah lives in San Francisco, "Then, like he said, rent a car and plan the trip from there."

"But I wanted this trip to be just us. Just our family."

"It would be, Matt, we'd just see Sarah and her family for a few days. I'm not going all the way out there without seeing them." I could feel my annoyance rising again. All the work I'd done to prepare and plan was starting to feel like a waste of time. It felt like, if I didn't act fast, the trip I wanted to take would morph into something entirely different.

"Oh, one more thing." Mr. Davis was back with a group of people, all with their coats on heading toward the door.

"Come on, Allen! Oh, hey, Matt," Mrs. Davis shouted over at our table.

"Hold on," he laughed. "This is important." Then he looked at me suddenly serious. "You talked just a second ago about journey and destination and all that, right? Well, looking at these plans it seems to me that you're *talking* about journey but your mind is on the destination."

"What do you mean?"

"The Big Trip. You've got to take 'The Big Trip.' That's your destination. As long as your focus is on the idea of The Big Trip you'll just be a tourist out there taking in the sights, just to see them, to say you did it." And here he paused to look at both of us. "You've got to know *why* you want to go. Once you've got that figured out, the *how* will take care of itself." Theresa and I looked at him in silence. "You guys take care," he said. Then he walked away.

Why did I want to go out West?

My friend John Shafer was fifty when he took his wife and two kids on a cross-country trip over the summer. He lost twenty pounds on the trip; said he felt like crap most of the time too. When he got home he went for his annual physical and after some tests they found he had pancreatic cancer. He was dead seven months later.

It's not enough to say, "Life is short." That's a bullshit cliché, because there are some times, maybe even *lots* of times that life feels hard and very long. I'd be lying if I said I've never thought of shortening it. Sometimes it just feels like too much. But the clock is always ticking. Given the way I've treated my body over the years, I bet I'm more than half way through. No way to be sure, but yeah, I'll say it, there's something about hitting the mid-life milestone that's behind why I wanted to go. Maybe part of it for me was about looking back while I still could.

But then I think about my kids.

I remember playing air guitar with Henry while listening to the Allman Brothers on full blast. Or pulling Max down from the magnolia tree in our front yard after he'd climbed nearly ten feet up when he was just barely able to walk. Or sneaking up on Harper dancing to music only she could hear in the living room, her own sweet drawings scattered at her feet.

Henry is on the cusp of high school now. Max is in middle school. And Harper can read all of the books I used to read her while she sat on my lap before bedtime, my nose in her fresh smelling hair.

Soon they'll be gone. Off living their own lives. I just want to give them something to remember us by.

And Us. Theresa and I. After all we've been through, if she had to do it over again, would she still choose me to take along on this journey? Would she choose this adventure? Sometimes, I'm not so sure. And I want her to say yes. Always yes. Maybe this trip would help.

My family is growing. My marriage is evolving. My career is . . . my career. And my country, my God, my country.

SOME nights, when I close my eyes at bedtime, I see myself standing in front of a card table covered with sweating, but empty glasses. And in my hands I'm holding one of those plastic pitchers you see at church potluck dinners. The pitcher is mostly full, but my hands are shaking and water is spilling over the sides. Every time I choose a glass and pour the water out, somebody comes and takes the glass away. And when I turn to fill another, I always find there are more glasses on the table than before, and I've got less and less water to fill them.

> *I went to the woods because I wished to live deliberately, to front only the essential facts of life, and see if I could learn what it had to teach, and not when I came to die discover that I had not lived.*
> — Henry David Thoreau

Through the Keyhole
(Days 1 and 2. Buffalo — San Francisco — Big Sur)

AFTER OUR PLANE CIRCLED Philadelphia three times, looking for a hole in the raging thunderstorm below that we might slip through to a safe landing, our redirected flight landed in Scranton. In a deep, reassuring voice, our pilot said, "The folks on the ground are already working on your changeover plans. We'll get you there safely and then have you headed out again to your next destination just as soon as we can."

Packed as we were like sweaty crayons in a Crayola box, Theresa and I smiled at each other over the seats. We knew there would be some hiccups on the trip; we just didn't expect one to happen on our first flight from home.

Knowing we had a long first day of travel ahead of us, I had gone over the itinerary with the kids in painstaking detail on the way to the airport, hoping that knowledge of what was to come would mitigate any anxiety they might have. As we approached Philly, Max was the first to notice we seemed to be circling. And after the pilot's announcement, all three of our kids looked over at us worried, it seemed, by the change of plans.

"No big deal, guys," I said. "We're safe and together. We'll get there eventually. The pilot seems like he's got everything totally under control." Which was not just some line of parental bullshit thrown out there to keep things calm. Admittedly, as a guy who is used to being in charge, I'm pretty slow to trust the competence of others, which can be both a good and bad thing. People generally need to *show* me I can trust them before I'm totally comfortable letting them run the show, but once they've earned that trust, they get the benefit of the doubt for a long time after. It's this character trait (flaw?) that's at least part of the reason I'm not a huge fan of flying; up there in the air, I'm not in control.

I don't know if it was because I was still running on the early adrenaline of the trip or if I heard something in the shrugged assurance of the pilot's voice that put me at ease, but once we landed, I was calm enough about our situation that I hung back with the kids and let the other passengers hustle to the ticket counter. We took our time disembarking, long enough to notice a praying mantis clinging to the plane's landing gear as we waited to grab our carry-ons from the luggage caddy. Having never seen one up so close, my kids were transfixed by the creature's huge eyes and menacing maw.

"See how its front legs bend up like that; like it's holding its hands in prayer? That's where it gets its name." Max made me take a picture. I called Henry over, "Hey, think about this: if we had run off crazy like the others, we'd never have seen the praying mantis. Pretty cool, huh?"

Henry, who was still worried about making the next plane, just shrugged. "Yeah, cool bug."

"You heard the pilot, bud. We'll probably just chill here for a bit and then get on another plane and be on our way. No worries. It'll work out." But as my last words of reassurance tumbled out of my mouth, I saw the man behind the authoritative voice that had given me such comfort on the plane. With a cluster of pimples where his five o-clock shadow should have been, the pilot waved to us on his way by, looking very much like he was rushing from tech class to get to study hall on time. "Hi, folks," he said. I swear his voice sounded at least two octaves higher in the open air. Now I was worried.

I guess by this point I should be used to it; kids less than half my age have been changing my car's oil for years now. To say nothing of the smartass millennial who spoke to us in the slow, patient way of a kindergarten teacher when Theresa and I set up our fancy new iPhones in 2017. (What? My flip-phone still worked at the time. Why did I need to get a new one?) But topping off all the fluids and explaining the limits of a chosen data plan are different things than flying a fucking airplane. Shouldn't an adult be doing this?

It's one of the weirdest parts of getting older: realizing people younger than you are more capable than you are. That'll humble you *fast*. But it goes the other way too. Just because a person is old, doesn't necessarily mean they're useless. Everybody has something to offer.

When my grandma was in the hospital dying from a slew of health complications, my mother made me take my grandpa, who had been sitting by her bedside without a break for days, down to the cafeteria to get him some lunch. My grandpa was one of these guys who liked his meat bloody. Like, literally. I remember watching him eat a handful of raw ground chuck as he slapped burgers together by the grill in his backyard. No lie.

And like me, my grandpa could be a rough-around-the edges pain in the ass, but he usually meant well. This time, shrunken somehow by his grief, I watched in disgusted awe as my grandpa tried to speak over the sizzle to a burger-flipping line cook in the hospital cafeteria. "Hey, flip that over for me, okay. Now just take it off. It's done. I like them rare." The guy just looked the other way and pushed the juice out of the puck-like patty with his spatula. It was as if my grandfather wasn't there.

The line cook didn't know a thing about my grandpa's life. He didn't know my grandpa had gone from living like a near-orphaned tramp as a child, to the athletic hall of fame at Colgate University. He didn't know my grandpa stormed the beaches of Okinawa in World War II and came home a hero, that he started from the bottom as a sales guy at IBM and retired a millionaire at fifty-five, only to work with his wife as a real-estate agent for another twenty years. No, all the line cook knew, with absolute certainty, was that there was some old guy bitching about his food like he knew better.

But here's the thing, I also get where the line cook was coming from. You spend most of your young life looking up to the people in charge and the people in charge are almost always older than you. Parents, grandparents, teachers, bosses, the like. They're the experts. They know what they're doing. But then at some point (and if you're lucky, this happens early) you realize that most of these so-called "adults" don't have the slightest clue either. They're just *people* like you, fumbling their way through. Fakin' it 'til they make it. But before you can tell everybody this great secret you've figured out, *you're* the adult and everybody's looking to you to lead the way. And you don't want to admit the most salient lesson life has taught you so far: just because you're in charge doesn't mean you know what you're doing.

"Here's your burger, *sir*. Well done, just like you like it. Next!" And to my astonishment, my grandpa just shuffled away.

The kids and I waited in the stiff, stuffed seats next to the ticket booth as Theresa stood in line trying to sort out our connecting flight. My guys are pretty patient in situations like these, thankfully slow to make a scene, but we were planning on eating lunch in Philly and that was an hour ago. Hunger is the mother of impatience. I explained there was a possibility that we would be re-boarding at a moment's notice and heading to Philly once the storm passed; I didn't want to head down the hall to the food court only to return and find we missed our flight. "But I'm hungry now," Harper complained.

"Hey, catch!" a bag of peanuts flew into Harper's lap. "I have cookies and pretzels too. Not a proper lunch, but it should hold you over until they finish refueling." The kid pilot was back. He waved over the rest of the passengers that hadn't already scurried onto other flights, and as he passed out the rest of the snacks to the gathering crowd said, "Looks like we've got a little window in the storm here, folks. The boys down below are fillin' her up, so if you'll quick gather your things and get back on board I should have us heading in the right direction in no time."

He got us to Philly with time to spare. Turns out the kid knew what he was doing after all.

AFTER eating overpriced, airport-knock-off Philly cheesesteak sandwiches, we were a long flight away from landing in San Francisco. It would be late when we got in (5:00 a.m. our time), but my brother-in-law, Greg, would be waiting up when the Uber dropped us off from the airport. There would be beds for us to crash in. And tomorrow, after I picked up the rental and we re-packed all of our things, it finally would be time for the trip to begin.

THERESA'S sister, Sarah, her husband, Greg and their three kids moved to the San Francisco area because of Greg's work a couple of years before we arrived out there to visit. They were renting a house in a hilly (of course) well-kept neighborhood not far from the airport, with spacious views of the bay off the back deck and a steady stream of planes flying overhead at all hours. Sarah was camping with the kids, so Greg greeted us when we got in and drove me to the rental car place the next morning on his way to work.

We flew with most of our gear (some of it borrowed from neighborhood angels who heard about our trip and were eager to help with advice and provisions) tightly packed into three huge duffle bags. But we also planned to borrow a bunch of stuff from Sarah and Greg, who are avid campers.

Though I picked up an adjunct class at a local private college to help fund the trip, and we had been putting all purchases on a credit card for months in an attempt to accrue airline miles, we knew there would be unexpected costs along the way. We didn't want to strictly tie ourselves to a tight budget, but we also didn't want to dig ourselves into a hole of debt we couldn't get out of when we all got back. So when it made sense we went with the cheapest option available. Which is why, even though we knew there would be days over the next three weeks where we would be driving for ten hours at a time, we arranged to rent a mid-range instead of a full-sized SUV; things would be cramped, but livable.

As Greg pulled out of the rental agency, a guy came out shaking his head. "Mr. Bindig, it looks like we've got a problem." A second trip hiccup already. This could not be good.

Once we decided to scrap the ten-week, June to August drive across the country plan in favor of flying out to Sarah's and renting a car to drive a nearly 4,000 mile figure eight loop through a handful of western states, we made arrangements to stay with some folks we knew along the way and also set reservations at various campgrounds, parks, Air BNBs, and a cool inn we found online. I built the trip's itinerary to resemble a cornfield: a clear sense of order and purpose that you could also get lost in. That said, like the red wheelbarrow, so much depended upon the vehicle. Without a trusty ride, all our plans would go out the window.

The rental car agent wiped his hands on his shirt. "Our mechanic was just looking over the vehicle you folks ordered and found that it's in need of some repairs. Nothing major, but it'll take at least a day to get the parts we need to fix it."

"A day? Sir, we can't wait a day," I said. "We've got reservations in Big Sur tonight."

"Well, we can always upgrade to the next size vehicle. We have one of those sitting right here," he pointed to a silver beast parked in the first bay of the garage. And immediately, I smelled a rat.

I get it, I thought. *The ol' bait and switch. Come on out west, boy. Build your dream trip around the idea that you'll be able to rent an affordable, reliable car, and then once your brother-in-law pulls away from the rental booth, you'll be stuck standing in a hot parking lot trying not to get screwed: either pay extra for a bigger vehicle or fuck up the first few days of your trip. The bastards always get you.*

"No extra charge, of course," the rental agent said.

"Excuse me?"

"It's our mistake. We should have checked it last night. Come on inside and we'll fill out the new paperwork for the Sequoia."

Maybe everything was about to change.

DRIVING along Route One is like riding a ribbon strung between Beauty and Fear. Ragged cliffs crash toward raging seascapes and endless vistas that stretch for miles to where blues blend into horizon-less possibilities. You can't help feeling like you're looking at drawings from God's Original Sketchbook. Curves and lines drawn back when the world was first becoming. It's like looking behind the curtain of Before-All-of-This. The Beauty.

But then there's also The Fear.

I steered the oversized rented sled, loaded with everything I hold precious in my life (well, not everything, Rosie the dog was staying at a "dog-camp" back at home for the duration of our trip) over blind turns on shoulder-less, cliff-edge roads, many of which lacked a guardrail. It took a while to figure out why so many of the cars that zoomed toward me, northbound and, therefore, on the mountain-side of the path, either swerved away or honked as they flew by. At first I thought it was because I was driving too slowly, so despite Theresa's steady flow of under-her-breath curses and admonitions, "Jesus! Matt!" "Shit, that was close!" "Slow down for God's sake! You don't know this car." I kept the pedal down to out pace my peers, even as my forearms burned and my hands cramped from gripping and turning the wheel with a sense of life or death purpose.

But when a sun-kissed guy in Ray Bans drove by in a red convertible (why is it always a *red* convertible) and shouted, "Move over, asshole!" I realized I was driving over the yellow-lined rumble strips in the middle of the road.

And here I thought, was the trip's first great metaphor. Being a parent is driving along the California coast. The whole ride you toggle back and forth between beauty and fear, hoping to drive in a way that'll allow you to appreciate the trip and also make it safely through. But here's the thing, if you stay in the middle of the road too long, somebody's bound to call you an asshole.

On one side you see the wonder. Your children. Lives brought into this world through your love and loins, unfolding in sometimes stumbling steps toward a sense of being that you, at least in part, get to design. They look like you, talk like you, and even sometimes *think* like you. And they possess your heart.

The bike seat leaves your steadying hand, outpacing your sprint as she straightens up and rides away along that first path toward freedom. Watching the game at night with a bowl full of chips on your lap and a sweaty can of beer in your hand, and he comes over and sits right next to you, thighs touching like when you used to read stories together in this same spot. Then he rests his eleven-year-old head against your shoulder, like it's nothing, like nothing has changed, even though tears fill your eyes with the joy of it. And lumpy Sunday morning pancakes and sausage proudly served to you from the skillet held in his small, trembling hand. The Beauty. The Beauty.

Then voices break in from the back. "Dad, Henry won't get off his phone!"

"Mind your own business, Max. Is that true Henry? I told you to put it away. We won't pass this way again."

"Max! Don't eat all the crackers on the first day! Mom! Max is eating all the crackers!"

"Harper, put those away."

"But, Mom, you said I could have them and Max keeps taking them from me!"

"Take care of it yourselves," Theresa rolls her eyes and looks out the window before flinching away as we round another bend. "Jesus, Matt! That was close. Watch what you're doing."

"Do I need to pull over and change seats, you guys? Come on."

"I'm not sitting in the middle. All my stuff is back here."

"Henry, is that helpful? And let's put the phone down, okay, and just look out the window, a bit? Isn't it beautiful?"

"It's been beautiful for hours, Dad. I'm just taking pictures to show my friends."

"Take pictures with your eyes. Life looks better from out behind a screen."

"Here we go."

It's just a stage, you tell yourself. Each of them is in a different stage. We've just got to love them through it. Show them The Beauty and they'll eventually come around. But then what if they don't? What if they turn out selfish and easily distracted, or become unwilling to help themselves even in the simplest of ways, what if rather than seeking consensus, they antagonize over ideals not really worth fighting for, become stubborn to a fault? What if they're too angry about an email to notice the sunset? Too sad about the news to gaze at the stars? What if they walk away from love because they've seen too much of what they care about crumble before their eyes? What if this life destroys their hope and spits them out empty and broken, grasping for meaning even before they're half way through?

What if they turn out just like me? The Fear.

"Why are we stopping?" Henry asked. "I thought you said we had another hour."

"The view, bud. Look at the view."

"Can't we just see it from the windows?"

"Come on, get out. Smell the air." Theresa, Max and Harper were already out of the car and standing with the wind in their hair looking out over the cliff's edge toward the blue beyond.

All along Route One there are these pull-offs where you can swing in to check out the scenery. The highway department probably put them in figuring if people stopped to get a good look and take some pictures, fewer people would plunge to their death because they spotted a passing pelican instead of keeping their eyes on the road. I pulled out my phone to take a few shots.

"I thought life looked better from out behind a screen, Dad."

When Henry was four years old, I spent the better part of two days creating alphabet cards for him. The letters (capital and lowercase) were in the upper left corner. In the middle I drew pictures of corresponding words. On "C" I drew a cat that looked just like our tabby, Smarty. On "H" I drew a picture of a cartoonish, blonde-haired, blue-eyed him.

When he was even smaller and got Salmonella from eating raw cookie dough and spent two days pooping his brains out only to find himself dehydrated and thus, ironically, constipated, it was *I* who put the suppository in. It was *I* who watched "Trashy Town," (the only kid-friendly VHS tape we owned because we didn't want our child watching violent anime cartoons), on repeat for hours while he clutched the edges of his training toilet with sweaty hands trying to make something come out. "Pick it up! Drop it down! Drive around in Trashy Town!" It was *I*.

Henry and I used to be best buddies. We walked together. Drew together. Read together. Teachers would pull me aside at open house and tell me how he'd told them he wanted to grow up to be just like his dad.

But now it's like he's always looking for me to falter, to contradict myself, to fall short — just so he can have the joy of pointing it out. I know full well I'm not perfect. Why is it so fun for him to tell me so? It's just a stage, right? But that doesn't make it suck any less. I don't have to be his best friend. In fact, I think it would be pretty weird if I were. I just don't want him to see me as useless.

"Uh, hey excuse me, sir." I turned away from the picture I was taking to find a college-aged kid and what I took to be his girl-friend standing next to The Sequoia's bumper by the side of the road.

"What's up?" I asked. The guy looked down.

"Just ask him, Justin." The girl implored.

"We, uh, we got a flat tire. Our car is the white one back there. I rented it for the day. Do you think you could help me? I don't know how to change it." His story bloomed in my head. Young, California kid. Wants to drive his girl along the rollercoaster coastline; give her a thrill. Maybe he's too poor to buy his own ride or maybe his own ride is a beater, so he rents this fancy white sports car for the day. Now he's got a flat, the car's due back by the end of the day and he's miles away from home and he doesn't know what to do.

Before I learned how to drive, my dad taught me how to change a tire. He made me do it over and over again in the driveway until I got it just right. It's a skill I'm glad to have because I've changed my own flat tire at least nine times in my adult life. I walked back with the kid to his car.

We opened his trunk and found the spare, the tire-iron and the jack. We put the parking brake on and I helped loosen the lug nuts. Henry was watching. Theresa was back in the car with Max and Harper getting another snack.

"Now what you've got to do is get the car up on the jack. Once you do that, you've got to take the flat tire off." I continued ex-plaining each of the steps. When I was done the kid handed me the jack as if he thought I was going to do it for him.

"Talk me back through the steps," I said. "You got this." He re-peated each of the steps I told him almost perfectly. "Good, now you know how to do it." His girlfriend smiled.

"I'll remind him if he misses anything," she said. "Thank you."

"Yeah, thanks." We shook hands and I wished them well. He was already putting the spare on as we pulled back onto the road.

We drove along in silence for a while. Then Henry spoke up. "Dad, why didn't you help that guy get the tire on?"

"Henry, your dad *did* help them. We were there for, like, ten minutes," Theresa said in my defense.

"It's cool, Theresa," I said. "Buddy, you saw. I helped him with the hard part and then talked him through the other stuff. He knew what he was doing by the time I left. Don't you think?"

"Yeah, I guess so," Henry said. "But why didn't you, you know, *do* it for him? Why didn't you just finish the job?"

"Good question. I guess there are two reasons." The car hummed along around another hairpin turn, tires squeaking as it went. "First, I want to make it to the campground so we can set up and have dinner before it gets too late. There's a beach I want to check out nearby. That's fair, right?" He nodded. "And second, changing that tire was *his* job, you know?" Henry just looked back at me through the rearview mirror. "Sometimes, when you're an adult, you've got to learn to give young people a chance to figure things out for themselves. Prepare them, yes. But then let them figure it out too."

"Oh. Okay. I got it, I guess," Henry said. Then he turned toward the window and watched as the ocean flew by.

Harper, Max and Henry — dancing with the Pacific. Pfeiffer Beach. Big Sur, California.

WE pulled into the Ventana Campground just after five o'clock and found our site nestled between two redwood trees. The forest floor felt soft and supple beneath our feet and the air was rich with the thick smell of cedar. Max and I set up the tent near the creek that laughed behind our spot while Henry and Harper helped Theresa unload the food we'd need for dinner and set up the camp stove. We ate a feast of hot dogs, macaroni and cheese, and sliced cucumbers while staring up at the trees around us.

After dinner we headed to Pfeiffer beach, a place I read about while researching the trip. Legend has it the sand there was purple and the rock formations were like miniature mountains rising out of the tide. Even though site after site warned us to stay out of the vicious undertows, I wanted to at least be prepared to swim if the warnings proved to be hyperbolic. So we changed into our bathing suits, grabbed our towels and drove to the winding dirt road that led to the shore.

We made our way down a path lined with sea-smoothed trees that looked like it belonged in the Garden of Eden. When the light broke through we found the beach curving away from the cliffs in a counterclockwise swoop. Aside from the roaring waves, the shore's most striking feature is Keyhole Arch — an impossibly square cavern cut through a just-off-shore rock formation by the knife of tide and time.

We walked together as a family down the beach over the violet sand and into the wind. When we'd put enough distance between us and the rest of those gathered along the shore, Theresa said, "No deeper than your waist." Then we sat down together to watch as our children danced in the sun-drenched waves.

Much later that night, as I lay on the ground almost three thousand miles from home, listening to the settled breathing of my sleeping family, the lingering light from Keyhole Arch flickered across my mind's eye. And as I fell asleep I thought of flat tires, and Henry, and the courage it takes to let the waves do their work.

Running Backwards
(Day 3. Big Sur — Santa Barbara)

A WEEK BEFORE WE departed for the trip, I asked Theresa for three days in seclusion to get things "fully organized." The plane tickets were purchased, couches to crash on coordinated, and our driving route chalked onto our dog-eared maps, but the granular details needed some attention. Knowing the nature of my neurosis, she agreed.

I spent my allotted hours alone scanning Trip Advisor, thumbing through AAA guidebooks, searching the pages of dusty National Geographics and canvassing the Internet to pool a list of cool stops and sights to see in between our trip's major destinations. Then, using the more linear trip itinerary I had already written as a scaffold, I wrote an eleven-page, single-spaced "Trip Narrative" outlining the plans, goals and possibilities of each of our twenty days away.

Now I am not blind to the fact that this "Trip Narrative" document could easily be used against me in a court of law. I can see it now: a collective counsel of Jack Kerouac, William Least Heat-Moon, and John Steinbeck move to quickly criminalize my work, recognizing it for what it is: an attempt to shackle the Freedom of the Road into a spreadsheet. Certainly our trip, cuffed as it now would be by my careful considerations, would lack the windows-down, wind-in your hair, "Ah, screw it, let's go!" spontaneity that drips from the dreams of American travelers who turn their eyes to The West. Fair points all.

But I am a "To Do List" person; I usually have two or three of them working at any given time. At different times in my life, I've created a four-paneled list by folding a sheet of paper, first horizontally and then vertically. In the upper left corner I'll write all the urgent things: *Grade English 11 quizzes and enter the scores into the grade book before 3:00 p.m. deadline*, the upper right corner is everything I need to do by the end of the week: *Take Henry to get new basketball shoes — try-outs are on Monday*. In the bottom left corner, I'll write stuff that needs to be addressed by the end of the month: *Schedule Rosie's annual vet visit*. And the bottom right corner will be things "On the horizon": *Clean the gutters before the snow flies*. Sometimes, if I do something that previously didn't appear on my "To Do List," I'll write it down on the list (in its proper place, of course) just so I can have the pleasure of then crossing it off. When the speaker of T.S. Elliot's, "The Love Song of J. Alfred Prufrock" says, "I have measured out my life in coffee spoons," I get what he means in a very personal way.

I know this is crazy. I wish I could live another way. But most mornings of my life feel like they've been tossed in a blender of have-tos and not-enough-time-fors. After the alarm rings, the dog gets walked, I shower, dress and eat, I'm lucky if I have five minutes to game-plan the afternoon with Theresa before I have to sprint off to work, where I'm inevitably slammed with emails to respond to, copies to make, and lesson plans to revise before the students start trickling in. Classes at my school start at 7:25 a.m.. The mindless hurry leaves me numb and disconnected from my own life. I'm lucky if I click out of autopilot by lunch. Maybe living a to-do list life is just my way of trying to gain some sense of control in a world that, more and more, feels like it's going off the tracks. Maybe it's just a survival mechanism. But when I woke up on the second day of our trip out West, everything felt different.

Max — straddling a campside creek. Ventana Campground. Big Sur, California.

THE day before, we intentionally set up our tent next to the small stream running through the campground. As I lay listening to the mingled sounds of my family's breathing and the water laughing over the rocks, I was struck by the fact that I was both conscious and still — two things that rarely happen simultaneously in my life anymore. After a few moments, I dug my journal out of my backpack and unzipped myself into the morning.

The sun slanted through the branches of the broad trees. Everything around me glowed with pause and purpose. Aside from the sounds of the stream, the world was perfectly silent. Here there were no messages, meetings, or traffic. Gone was the busy bustle of earning a living. No phones clicked, buzzed or tweeted. The stillness was holy. So I turned to a crisp, clean page in my journal and began to write about the man I saw running backwards.

WE passed Shadrack Anderson Jr., The Backwards Running Man, on the shoulder of the road somewhere between San Francisco and our campsite in Big Sur. An RV rolled along a few hundred yards ahead of him emblazoned with a collection of advertisements from companies apparently sponsoring his quest. He was sweaty and shirtless and moving with a grace and efficiency that seemed impossible given he was running ass-first into the wind. The sight of a super fit, seventy-something dude running backwards along the edge of a cliff was compelling enough to send me searching on my phone. That's where I found Ashlyn Rollins' article from *The Half Moon Bay Review* in which the earnest writer explains the details.

Apparently when Anderson returned from his service in Vietnam, he claims he entered a trance where "backward running discovered him." So now he's attempting to run this way from the coast of California to New York City in an attempt "to bring something positive" to the world. I'm not exactly sure how those pieces fit together, but the metaphor was pretty clear to me. Making progress is one thing, but if your eyes and heart are facing the wrong direction aren't you sort of, you know, *missing the whole point of the trip*? He might be the one with all the sponsors, but Shadrack Anderson Jr. ain't the only American running backwards.

WE made good time as we drove from Big Sur to Santa Barbara. Hurtling past coastal scenes, the fear and excitement of Highway One's rollercoaster turns now familiar enough to feel a bit benign. When we passed Salinas, I played the kids both Janis Joplin's and Johnny Cash's live versions of "Me and Bobby McGee" to see which one they liked better. Joplin's won in a landslide, through I'm partial to the way Cash sings "was blowin' sad while Bobbie sang the Blues."

When we passed a sign for Soledad, I told them about Steinbeck and how I always take my classes outside to sit underneath a willow tree as I read aloud the last chapter from, *Of Mice and Men*.

The California hills are drought-ridden, dry and dusty. We drove past workers, blurry in the heat that swirled out from behind their machines — their callouses different from mine. There is an America many of us never get to see.

Just after we passed San Simeon, from the road, Theresa saw two enormous Elephant Seals doing battle in the surf. We pulled over into the visitor center where we found a sizable parking lot and plenty of space to view the seals. We stood with the other folks behind the guardrails, snapping pictures and videos as the boisterous males slammed their bodies into each other. "Why are they fighting?" Harper asked, her nose crinkled like her mom's.

"Just trying to show off for the girls," Theresa said.

"Yeah, everybody's got something to prove," I laughed. Henry scoffed. Max, who is the type of kid who would try to climb a telephone pole while walking down the street in New York City (this actually happened once) had one leg over the fence, his eyes aglow at the possibility of communing with a 1,600 pound seal. "Max, get back here. Can't you read the sign?"

"But I want to see them."

"You can see them from here."

Together we read the posted signs that, in addition to warning against close encounters with the seals, explained their migratory habits and molting patterns.

The beach to our left was covered in what we thought were huge boulders until some of them began moving and we realized they too were seals, close to one hundred in total, females and their young clustered together in the sun.

"Did you know this was here, Dad?"

"No, Harper, we just found it. Mom saw the seals fighting. That's why we stopped."

"Good thing she was looking, huh? That was so cool."

"Yeah, Lulu. Good thing she was looking."

We arrived in Santa Barbara at four o'clock — about an hour before we told Theresa's Cousin, Joe and his wife, Angela, we'd show up — so I pulled The Sequoia into a park next to the Santa Barbara pier. We changed into our bathing suits behind half-open doors in the parking lot and headed for the water. Though the kids swam the night before, I had only gone in up to my knees. I wanted to feel the Pacific around my shoulders.

The kids and I walked along the rocky shore and swam out a bit into the frigid water. Then we walked out on the long pier. Even though the sun was still high, the air had a bite to it we could feel as the water whisked off our skin. We changed again, and then followed Joe's directions from the main drag to his house.

Theresa's parents valued family and made a point of regularly taking trips to visit their relatives, but when Joe's mother, Maryann, divorced Theresa's uncle, Jim, and moved to the other side of the country, that branch of the family grew distant. Though we planned to sleep in their house that night, Theresa had never actually met her cousin Joe, his wife Angela or their two kids. As someone who was raised only seeing my aunts, uncles and cousins at holiday gatherings or rare summer barbeques, showing up from Buffalo with our three kids hoping to crash at their place seemed like a big ask. But Theresa made the arrangements and assured me it would be fine.

We slowly rolled down the street looking for the house number and eventually pulled a U-turn to head back; we missed it the first time. When we saw the house, we parked on the other side of the street and prepared to disembark. By the time our doors were open, a man was briskly walking toward our car from across the lawn.

"Are you lost?" he barked. Then he lowered his voice to just above a whisper and said, "Make sure you lock the doors. There's been a lot of drug activity in the neighborhood lately."

I was about ready to get back into the car when Theresa said, "Hey, Joe, you look just like a Weidmann!" And as soon as she said it, I saw the family resemblance as well. Joe cracked into a smile and gave her a hug. He grabbed our bags from our hands and ushered us into the house, leaving the front door wide open behind him as he went.

When Theresa and I were dating and I'd show up to see her, in answer to my knock, her father would regularly open the door about six inches and say, "I gave at the office!" before slamming it shut again, leaving me to stand awkwardly on the stoop for a minute or two, not really sure if I should knock again or what. He had a pretty weird sense of humor. Maybe it runs in the family.

Within a half an hour though, I felt like I'd known these people my entire life. Angela showed us back to the garage, which was converted to a guest apartment complete with full bath and laundry facilities. She was funny and engaging as she showed us around, completely at ease with herself. And she drew my kids out right away — talking to them about school and the trip and what they liked to do for fun.

Angela and Joe's kids, Jackson and Adella, are the type of young people who look adults in the eye and stick around to be part of the conversation. Jackson took the kids and me back to his workshop to show us a 3D printer he set up. It was buzzing away, making a small part for a machine of some sort that he was building. Turns out he graduated from high school early and was attending a local community college to get a start on credits. Adella sat with us at the dining room table and looked through an old photo album, showing Theresa pictures of her aunt and uncle from before she was born.

Maryann (Joe's mother, Theresa's aunt) showed up with her oldest daughter, Jean, and together the whole group jumped into cars and headed to the waterfront for dinner. We sat in the street and devoured savory fried seafood. Maryann passed her plate to us, insisting we share, and she picked up the bill as well.

After dinner we walked as a group along another pier. Max climbed up and down the rocks, spotting sea creatures and hidden treasures. While Henry, Jackson, Joe and I paced out in front, Theresa and Harper walked behind with the other ladies.

One of the things that drives my kids crazy about me when we travel, is I'm always starting conversations with strangers. If I see a guy pumping gas in Pennsylvania while wearing a Minnesota Vikings hat, I'm likely to say something like, "How's a guy from Pennsylvania come to like the Vikings? I thought everybody in this part of the state was a Steelers fan?" It's a habit that's led to more than a few good stories over the years, but Henry, in particular, hates it. It *embarrasses* him. But so what, he's thirteen; *everything* I do embarrasses him.

But this night I was impressed with Henry as he walked along with the older guys. He must have thought Joe and Jackson were pretty cool because he was talking freely to them, joking a little, even asking a few questions of his own. Maybe I didn't embarrass him as much as I thought.

The sun was quickly setting and the temperature dropped in kind. When you're from the Buffalo area and you think of California you instantly think of palm trees and surfers, but in the shadow of the mountains, Santa Barbara was *cold*. I was ready to head back, I knew we had a long day of driving ahead of us tomorrow, but when I said so, Maryann cut in.

"Before we head back to the house, we've got one more stop to make." She nodded, almost solemnly. "McConnell's. Best ice cream around." All of the natives in the group smiled in agreement.

We drove to the other side of town and stood in line outside of an ice cream shop right out of the movies. The walls were lined with photos of famous folks all enjoying their favorite homemade flavor. When the other customers around our group overheard we were from out of town, more than a few of them insisted we try a particular flavor they deemed the best.

I was near the front of the line with Maryann and Harper and when I went to pay, Maryann once again insisted on treating the entire party. Harper and I got our cones and headed out to the parking lot to wait for the others to join us.

The place was packed, so it took a while for everyone to get back to the cars, but I didn't mind. It was nice to stand there in the middle of a strange city eating ice cream with my daughter. How many times would this kind of thing happen again? The light from the shop lit up the scene, and from where I stood I saw Theresa joking with Joe, Max picking out his flavor with Adella, Jean and Angela chatting back and forth with Henry and Jackson, and Maryann, looking over the group with pride.

I live less than a mile from my brother. I bet if you totaled the number of words he's said to my children in their lifetimes it wouldn't fill a page of this book. I'm not complaining, just saying, you can spend your whole childhood living with someone only to find out later they really couldn't care less about you. Then again, you can fly across the country, take a walk with some total strangers and by the end of the night feel completely at home. "Family" is a word with a thousand definitions.

WHEN we returned to the house, Joe walked us back to where we were staying. He showed us how to work the washing machine and how to turn on the shower. As he was leaving, I noticed some band equipment set up in the corner of the garage.

"Yeah, I play with some guys every now and then," Joe admitted. "It's fun," he shrugged. "Just one of those things you do to stay alive." Then he said goodnight.

WHEN I was a little kid, my dad had a guitar he used to bring out and play in the living room after dinner. Sometimes he played songs by himself, sometimes he'd have my brother and me sit with him while he taught us songs to sing. I remember one time, my dad taught us "Annie's Song" by John Denver while we helped him do the dishes and my mom took the dog for a walk around the block. Then, when my mom came home and jumped in the shower, we practiced singing the newly learned lyrics while my dad played along on the guitar.

> *You fill up my senses.*
> *Like a night in the forest.*
> *Like the mountains in springtime.*
> *Like a walk in the rain.*
> *Like a storm in the desert.*
> *Like a sleepy blue ocean.*
> *You fill up my senses.*
> *Come fill me again.*

The three of us sang to her that night. I can still see my mom sitting there in her blue bathrobe with her wet hair tossed all around her shoulders.

As my brother and I grew older, my dad played his guitar less and less. I never really understood why because he always seemed so happy when he played. I liked singing along with him too. When Todd entered high school he started pulling away from the family. Not in the usual ways either, he was pretty mean about it. He said some awful things back then, especially to my dad. But then one day, Todd asked my dad if he could have his old guitar, the one we used to sing John Denver songs on together; he said wanted to learn how to play it himself. And my dad gave it to him. Just like that.

THERESA'S dad was an old-school-Catholic. Church and family were the dual centers of his life. So it was a big deal that he went to Notre Dame to be an architect. But architecture school at Notre Dame is pretty tough. Ray was a hard working guy. It says something about the place that by his sophomore year, Ray was back home in Rochester attending St. John Fisher College and studying to become an accountant.

He told me all of this one time when I was helping him clean the gutters in the back of his house. My father-in-law was a proud man, but he didn't seem ashamed of flunking out of Notre Dame — just said it matter-of-factly. "But why didn't you stick with architecture?" I asked. "When you went to Fisher, I mean."

"Well, Matt," he said, "I would have been a very poor architect. When I got home from Notre Dame, my father told me so. But I was always good with numbers. So that's what I did."

For most of his adult life, Ray owned his own business. He did taxes and managed investments for people. He earned enough to keep up a large home and help send his five kids to private colleges. He was a tireless worker, but it never really seemed like he enjoyed it very much. Most times when I was over, he'd be off in his office, working until dinner, and many times he'd go back to it after the meal — making calls and crunching numbers into the night.

When he died and we were cleaning out his office, we found a collection of drawings tucked behind his desk. Some were clearly from his college days — a large poster depicting a modern house and its layout — but others were just as clearly more recent. Landscape drawings of the berm and entryway he eventually added onto the side of the house, sketches of buildings I didn't recognize, a cottage looking over a lake. Maybe that's what he was working on in his office all those evenings. Drawing pictures in his mind when nobody else was watching. Just one of those things you do to stay alive.

I sat up alone long after Theresa and the kids were asleep, looking on as Joe's band equipment reflected back the scant California light through the cracks in the curtains, thinking about the fathers in my life.

It's hard to hear your own heart over the howling roar of the crowd. And when you do hear it, it takes courage to listen and conviction to follow.

Joy is a fleeting, precious thing. You can find it in a stumbled upon pack of seals, old songs sung together, a cold unexpected swim or ice cream cones shared with strangers turned into family. But it's also there in the dreams we keep quiet, the things we keep just for ourselves, and all the *what-could-have-beens*. There is power in those refusals too. Power, sadness, *and* joy.

This is There
(Day 4. Santa Barbara — Los Angeles — San Diego)

THE FRIDAY BEFORE SPRING Break 2017, I shook every one of my seniors' hands as they walked out of class, making sure to make full eye contact. I wished each of them good luck and told them, "Be well." I lingered with a handful of the best writers and encouraged them to always use their voices for good. Many of them looked at me quizzically and a few even asked "What's up?", but I just nodded their questions away and smiled. I knew I was betraying them. I knew I wouldn't be seeing many of them ever again.

Three weeks before, I arranged a meeting with my administrators and tearfully told them I either needed to take a leave of absence for the rest of the year or resign my teaching position. Things had come to that. To their credit, my principal and vice principal sat with me long after our scheduled time, listening and even shedding a few tears of their own as I told them about the downward spiral of my emotional well-being. I was broken, unable to feel joy. My rich and meaningful life felt hollow and empty. I needed help. I didn't even know if I wanted to live anymore.

The next week, I received a formal diagnosis of clinical depression (turns out I wasn't just a melting snowflake, crushed by the election) and arrangements were made with the school district for me to take a sabbatical for the rest of the academic year.

I did not want to go on medication, but agreed to attend bi-monthly therapy sessions to try to address my symptoms. Eventually my doctor convinced me to try daily doses of CBD oil as well.

At my request, the administrative team agreed to not make the arrangements public until my leave commenced. I didn't want to have to face any questions from students, parents or colleagues. I was ashamed of what I had become, which is crazy because nobody feels ashamed when they get cancer, they just go about getting the help they need with the support of the community. Why should mental health be any different?

The 2016-2017 school year was particularly stressful for many of my students. For most of the fall the country seemed on the brink of civil war. After the election, a cloud of uncertainty hung over everything. Some teachers (the ones with "Build the Wall" bumper stickers tacked up behind their desks) gloated their way through the halls. Others wore funeral suits and handed out free copies of The Constitution to every kid who passed their door on the day Obama handed over the keys to the kingdom to our newly hailed slumlord-in-chief. Kids look to the adults in their life to be a steadying force. Instead I was leaving them at the time they needed me most. But I either needed to save them or save myself. I couldn't do both. Not this time.

After the students left, I wrote all of them an email letting them know I wouldn't be returning for the rest of the school year. I didn't explain why, I just said good-bye. I wrote a similar message to their parents. Then I sent a final note to my colleagues.

I knew the cost of not being more forthcoming was likely a swirl of rumors and innuendo. After all, usually when teachers go on leave like this it's because they've done something *wrong* (a D.W.I. arrest, embezzling club funds, messing around with a student). I tried to craft my notes in such a way to make it both clear and believable that my leave was not disciplinary in nature, but urgent nevertheless. Then I packed up my things and took the back stairway down to the side door that leads to the faculty parking lot. When I pulled away, I didn't look back.

"THINGS weren't always easy for me growing up; I learned early that if you show or admit weakness, people will pounce on it and try to destroy you. It's weird, people tell me all sorts of personal stuff all the time. Maybe because they see me as a pretty accepting guy. I'm not prone to instant, damning judgment. And I can admit when I'm wrong. I don't *like* to do it, but I can when it's obvious and I have no other choice. And I'm not afraid to apologize. So people trust me. They let me into their lives. I don't have a lot to hide. I've been through some things I don't really like talking about, but it's not like I have these deep, dark secrets. That said, I like it when people get to know me *on my terms*. I guess what I'm saying is I have a very hard time trusting other people. They've got to *earn* my trust. And since I'm paying you to listen to me, I probably will never really trust you. No offense. I'm sorry if I seem defensive or whatever. I just don't trust therapists."

This is how I started my first session with Maria. This is how I answered when she asked, *So what brings you in today?*

"Why don't you trust therapists?"

"Well, like I said, I'm paying you to care. Plus my Mom's a therapist."

Maria raised an eyebrow; a non-verbal tick I would come to know meant she was inviting me to say more. But when I didn't, she asked, "And what does your mother being a therapist have to do with it?"

"Well, I love my mom and all, it's just sometimes she doesn't see reality the same way I do. Let's put it that way," I said.

"So because you and your Mom see things differently, and she's a therapist, you don't trust therapists?"

"Right."

"Doesn't that seem like a big jump? Isn't it possible that some therapists are trustworthy?"

"Of course, of course, that's obviously true. I just don't think this will help me."

"Then we're back to my first question again," Maria nodded, looking down at the pad where she was jotting down periodic notes. "Why are you here?"

"Well, it's just that I have this great life and lately I don't really feel like being part of it."

"Why not?"

"That's what I'm trying to figure out, and I've only got three months to do it."

"Why only three months?"

"Well that's when my leave is up and I've got to decide whether or not I can go on teaching and living my life as I've always planned or if it's time to just crumple all of that up and, you know, just say 'fuck it.'"

"No pressure," she smiled.

THE second time I showed up at Maria's office I came with a calendar and two lists. The first list was full of things I knew I needed to do to more of in order to feel better: exercise, read for pleasure, write, maintain consistent sleep patterns, have regular sex, spend meaningful time with my children, drink less, make healthy food choices, get outside every day, listen to music, minimize my interaction with technology, stay on top of my work commitments, spend unscheduled time with Theresa, and make time for silence in my life.

The second list was all of the things I wanted to do when I was on leave: learn to play the guitar, take yoga classes, lose fifteen pounds, run everyday, start my next book, get off of Facebook, research getting a new puppy, and go to New England to visit some friends I haven't seen in a few years.

The calendar, charted out, in both macro and micro orientations, how I was going to spend my time. Guitar lessons every Tuesday. Yoga class in the mornings three times a week after I finished my run. You get the idea.

"May I see those?" Maria asked, indicating both the lists and the calendar with another arched eyebrow.

"Yes, I brought them to show you. This way at the end of our time, whenever that is, we'll be able to see if I've made progress."

She smiled and held out her hand. When I passed the papers over to her she said, "Let's talk about progress."

In American life everything is transactional. Everything is commodified. Progress is all about where you're going. The destination. How much have you moved the needle from the starting point of the previous generation? Everybody knows the script. It's finish line thinking. "Once I achieve X, then I'll be happy."

This is why so many kids cheat their way through school these days. In their minds, it doesn't matter if they actually *learn* anything so long as their report card sparkles with high 90s at the end of the year. It's the high 90s that get you into college, not your ideas. Getting into a good college will help you earn a marketable degree. A marketable degree will help you get a good job, with a decent starting salary and reasonable benefits. Then you can buy a fancy car, and later, a house in a nice neighborhood with decent schools and regular garbage pick-up. Once you've got those things it'll be easy to find a spouse who'll laugh at your dumb jokes while you walk on the beach together on one of the several vacations you take each year. Livin' the dream. It's all about the finish line.

But the more I live, the more I realize how toxic all this finish line thinking really is. There's a lot of living to be done in between the chalked lines of the start and finish. And you can miss it if all you're thinking about is jumping over life-hurdle after life-hurdle chasing a shining resume or whatever.

I have not always known this to be true, but I do now, and a lot of the reason why is what happened to us on the day we drove from Santa Barbara to San Diego by way of Los Angeles.

WE enjoyed a sun-drenched breakfast with Joe and Angela on their back patio, talking about school and kids and parenting. Theresa's family is notorious for their long, slow good-byes. Seriously, at whole-family gatherings, it can take three different rounds of hugs and well-wishes before people finally get in their cars and pull out of the driveway. Sometimes even after three rounds we'll sit with the car running and the windows down talking for another fifteen minutes before we finally go. I'm more of a "Love ya, bye" kind of guy.

But Theresa's friend Emily was expecting us in San Diego (almost four hours away by the way we drew up the map) for dinner and we wanted to spend at least a couple of hours in LA on the way, so I gave Joe and Angela two copies of my novel (one for them and one to pass on to Jean and Maryann), thanked them for taking us in and headed out once again for the coast.

THE theme song for the summer of 2019 (at least among middle schoolers in the Buffalo area) was Lil Nas X's, "Old Town Road" featuring burnt out quasi cowboy, Billy Ray Cyrus (he, formally of the woeful mullet). I spent many of the later days of my youth listening to Public Enemy, Dr. Dre, and Cypress Hill at deafening volumes while driving down neat suburban streets in my father's minivan, so I guess I can understand both the irony and the teenage urge to listen to music that doesn't have any sort of meaningful connection to your life, but at least the music I listened to back then was, you know, *good*. Anyway, by the time we hit the coast I'd heard "Old Town Road" played in full, at the kids' insistence, three times on three different radio stations. What the hell?

And it's because of the third verse of this little, regrettable ditty (sung by the mullet himself) that my boys were particularly excited about driving through Beverly Hills. More specifically, "Ridin' down Rodeo in [our] Maserati sports car." Never mind that we were "ridin'" in a silver Toyota Sequoia packed to the gills with camping gear and bagged lunches.

I'm not sure if it was his recently discovered excitement about Beverly Hills or the fact that it was his turn to be banished to the windy backseat of The Sequoia while his siblings played travel checkers together that prompted Max to pepper our ride from Joe and Angela's to the City of Angels with endless variations of the most annoying question ever asked of a parent from the backseat, but it was really irritating either way.

"Are we there yet?"

"When are we going to get there?"

"How much longer, Dad?

"Mom, can you ask your phone how many more miles?"

As we entered the city, a stream of cars dammed up in a coagulated mass of congestion in front of us, and Max let out a desperate cry. "We're never going to get there!" Something about the absolute, fearful urgency in his voice pushed me over the edge.

"This is there, Max! This. Is. *There*." The car fell silent.

"What?"

"*This* is where we are going," I said.

"A traffic jam? I thought we were going to see Hollywood?"

"No, not a traffic jam, Max." Then I reconsidered, fumbling for words to communicate what I suddenly realized was an essential truth. "*This*," I said and swept my arm across the windshield's wide view. "Our trip isn't just about the places we're going — it's about the getting there too: the journey."

I turned around for a moment to fully face Max. Henry and Harper stopped playing their game.

"Turn around, Matt! Watch where you're going." Theresa grabbed my shoulder.

"I am watching where we're going," I said, pointing toward the kids.

"What are you talking about?"

I turned back to face the road and said, "Look at that man sitting in the car next to us, Max." I pointed out the window to a guy eating a bagel with one hand, and holding his phone against his ear with his shoulder as he steered his baby blue BMW through the smog-infested traffic. "That guy there," I pointed again for emphasis, "is a person you'll probably never see again in your whole life. In a second, traffic's gonna pick up and we'll speed off toward Beverly Hills and he'll speed off to wherever it is he's going. But for this one second we're *here*. Next to each other. For this one second, we can *look* at each other and *notice* each other. You've got to see that kind of thing, Max. That's what life is about. There is *beauty* in that. There is *beauty* in the journey." Max looked into my eyes in the rearview mirror from the far back of The Sequoia. "This is there. *This* is where we're going. You get it?"

"Hey, what the fuck are you pointing at, asshole?" The guy in the BMW pulled up next to us and was shouting over his passenger seat while continuing to crawl along, one eye on the traffic in front of him.

"No, I was just making a point to my kid," I said. "No worries, Bud." But he drove away while I was still talking. Drove away before I could explain to him about the beauty.

IT was just after noon when we finally found a place to park and began walking toward Rodeo drive. Beverly Hills was *hot*. Theresa and the kids wanted to check out the scene, but I was hungry and wanted to find a place to eat.

"Let's look for a Jamba Juice, Dad," Henry said.

"What's Jamba Juice?" I asked

Henry stopped and struck a mid-crouch pose and began waving his hands back and forth in front of him like he was scratching records on a turntable. "Now it's four a.m. and I'm back poppin with the crew, I just landed in, Chase B mixes pop like Jamba Juice." He stopped rapping just as quickly as he started and began walking once again down the street as I stood behind him looking on in bewildered wonder. "Travis Scott," he said over his shoulder. As if that explained everything.

I walked behind my family watching as Henry snapped pictures of passing sports cars, Max pointed out storefronts of businesses I never knew he'd heard of before, and Harper gawked at outfits you would never see in Buffalo.

"What's the matter, sweetie?" Theresa squeezed my hand.

"It's hot and I hate all this," I said.

"Come on, try to be a good sport."

"I'm hungry."

"We're walking to get some food. Try to enjoy this, okay."

"What is *this*, anyway?"

"*This*," she said smiling, "is there."

Max, Henry and Harper — catching rays in front of the lily pond. Beverly Gardens Park. Beverly Hills, California.

HENRY was stopped on the corner, about ten yards in front of us, pointing urgently to a large pink and melon building whose white arches dwarfed the palm trees that swayed in the wind next to it. "Louis Vuitton!" he said.

"What's so big about Louis Vuitton?" Harper asked hopefully.

"When Charlie was in New York City, he got this cool Louis Vuitton wallet. Turns out it was a knock-off, but this is a Louis Vuitton *store*. I can get the real thing."

"Henry, Louis Vuitton makes women's handbags," I said.

"And wallets. Come on, can we go in?"

"No, you already have a wallet.

"*Dad!*"

"Come on, Henry," Theresa spoke up by my side. "We can go in."

"You're going to go look at a bunch of women's handbags with him?"

"And wallets!" Henry said.

"It *could* be fun," Theresa said, rolling her eyes. "The kids and I will just check it out. Are you going to wait out here?" In a flash I saw a future therapy session in which a now-adult Henry was talking to some shrink about how his *dad* never let him do anything he wanted to do as a kid. How his *dad* never accepted him for who he really was. How his *dad* . . .

"Hold on, I'm coming," I said.

WE rounded into the building and were directed by a sign to stash our bags at the coat check. A tuxedoed guard stood waiting to serve us. He took my daypack, loaded with water bottles and snacks and gave me a slip of paper for its return. Then he looked me up and down, a slight smile on his face. Maybe it was my knee-length cargo shorts he objected to (whatever, the pockets are great for storing things) or the performance camp shirt I wore: short-sleeved, collared, SPF 50 rated that gave him pause (whatever, my clothes were practical, which is more than I could say for him). "The exhibits are around the corner," He said. "The tour is self-guided."

"Tour? My son's looking for a wallet."

"This is not a store, sir, this is a mus*eum*."

"A museum of what?"

"The *art* of Louis Vuitton!"

Theresa was next to me again with five ticket stubs in her hands. "I guess it's a museum, babe. The kids still want to see it though, so I just went ahead and bought the tickets."

"How much for the tickets?"

"Only ten bucks each," she shrugged.

"Fifty bucks to see the *art* of opulence?"

She crinkled her nose and shrugged. "The brochure says Lady Gaga's Oscar dress is here. Come on."

"Whatever."

To be fair, the place was pretty interesting in an I-don't-give-a-shit-about-this-sort of-thing kind of way. I mean I've had really smart people I love and care about tell me that fashion *inspires* them, and I guess I can see it. Clothes are a human expression, just as much as these words are. There's a utility to what I'm doing here just as there's a utility to my SPF 50 rated camp shirt. And the beauty I was talking to Max about on the highway, well, I guess that was there in the Louis Vuitton museum too. Maybe.

After we finished our tour, we found a place to order some food. It cost $123.67 for the five of us to eat avocado toast, hummus and the like, but they wrapped it up neatly for us in brown paper bags and we walked back up Rodeo drive, carrying our lunches like hobos toward a little park we'd seen on the way in by a fountain near the iconic Beverly Hills sign. I didn't realize I knew about that sign until I saw it. But when it came into view, I was all like "Look kids, the famous Beverly Hills sign!" It's amazing what seeps into your brain. You can't ever keep all that shit out, even if you try.

TIME was going faster than we thought it would. Emily would be waiting for us with dinner in San Diego, which was still a pretty good drive away. We'd need to be strategic if we hoped to see the things we wanted to see.

We found a lunch spot in the shade on the roots of an amazing tree in Beverly Gardens Park. The kids climbed the low branches, bellies full of over-priced food, while Theresa and I got to work. Tossing previously desired destinations over our shoulders, we sketched out a route on the map that took us past the Hollywood Walk of Fame and The Dolby Theatre. If we were lucky we'd catch a glimpse of the Hollywood sign as well.

We spent the next hour navigating city streets in a drive-by tour that was the definition of an inch deep and a mile wide. I'm not even sure why it mattered to me to see those things. I like the movies and all, but Hollywood culture kind of drives me crazy too. Maybe I just wanted to be able to *say* I'd been there. Which made me think: maybe Henry's desire to get a *real* Louis Vuitton wallet so he could show Charlie wasn't so stupid after all. We're all just victims of osmosis.

THE ride out of L.A. was hard. Five lanes, bumper-to-bumper, incessant horns, and homeless people huddled together in make-shift campsites under overpasses strewn with trash. Having read *Blue Highways* a month before we left Buffalo, I was determined to avoid expressways on the trip, but Theresa was tired and so were the kids, and like I said, we had a long way to go. She begged me to get in the fast lane.

A month before Theresa and I got married, I asked a buddy of mine whose marriage I respected, what the secret was to marital bliss. "Lots of people say a good relationship is 50/50," he said. "That's bullshit. It's got to be 90/10."

"I don't get it," I admitted.

"90/10," he repeated. "Each person in the couple has to feel like they're carrying 90 percent of the load. In a relationship, if *both people* go into it thinking they've got to carry 90 percent, well, that's the recipe for a long happy marriage, my friend."

Good advice.

We compromised; I gave up seeing USC and the Coliseum and took the expressway through the city. Once outside of city limits though, I worked us back toward Route One, where the ocean views and winding roads worked their magic on my strained shoulders and city-soaked soul. Before long, I was whistling into the wind of the rolled-down window as we cruised past Huntington Beach.

We got out for a bathroom break at a bagel joint in Newport Beach. The water looked like heaven. Road weary, we decided to take a walk through a neighborhood, just to stretch our legs. Have you ever stopped to think about all the other lives you might have lived? One choice here or there and everything could be different? Not better, just different. Newport Beach, California, man. Choose your own adventure.

But then again sometimes your adventure chooses you. Sometimes it's out of your hands. That's what I was thinking anyway, as we arrived at Emily's just before dinner.

Blessing the Stars
(Day 5. San Diego — Joshua Tree)

WHEN WE HAD FINALIZED our route along the coast, Theresa insisted we include a stop at her friend Emily's. Theresa and Emily have known each other since they were First Years in college. As their respective adult lives unfolded, both made efforts to stay connected beyond college reunions and social media sharings.

For several years after college, Emily lived relatively close by in Connecticut. But after her youngest son, Hudson, died from complications at birth, she moved back to the San Diego area to live with her father and her oldest son, Harrison, in the house she grew up in. Hudson's death was the final straw for her already strained marriage; she and her husband divorced. I guess Harrison doesn't get to see his father very often. The man doesn't seem to have much interest in being a dad. Sad as that is, after the way he's treated Emily, it's okay with me if he stays as far away as possible. She deserves better and so does her son.

I've known Theresa since she was eighteen. What's funny about loving someone that long is after a while their friends become your friends too. I've always enjoyed spending time with Emily. Her easy laugh and full-spirit earned her fast friendships with a wide array of people in college. And her big, beautiful eyes and endless waves of blonde curls drew the interest of more than a few of my football teammates. But she's more than just fun and pretty; she's smart too. Like me, she works in schools, and even though she spends her time with younger kids, I've always found her insights about education to be both well refined and useful for me to consider when thinking about my own classroom. I was really looking forward to seeing her.

Harper and Harrison are about the same age, so as we walked up to the front door, I did my best to pump her up for meeting him; she sometimes can be shy at first. The door swung open and Harrison burst out. "They're HERE!" he shouted. Then he pulled my kids around the house showing them toys and rooms and the TV show he liked to watch best. Emily took Theresa into the back-yard, while I carried our bags in from the car.

To his credit, Henry led the kids in a pick-up game of soccer as Emily, Theresa and I put a quick dinner together and caught up over a glass of wine. As we worked to prepare the meal, I couldn't help noticing Emily was dripping with sweat. I mean, just-ran a 5K dripping. When I asked her about it she explained that the condition that had led to Hudson's early birth, caused her blood pressure to skyrocket. She had almost died. Deprived as it was of oxygen, her body almost shut down, frying her nerves' circuit board in the process. She was alive, though it had been close, but now all sorts of weird things happened with her body. Like sweat-ing all the time. "It's just me now, I guess." She laughed but I felt a sudden stab of something behind her smile. There was a sadness just below the surface of everything there.

"I'VE got a date tomorrow," she told us. "I met him online. It's my first date since the divorce." Theresa and Emily talked about the details as the kids poured in from outside. They gobbled up the food we prepared almost as fast as we plated it.

I had never met Emily's father before, and just like with Joe and Angela, I felt weird about showing up on his doorstep with my kids and camping gear, and asking to spend the night. From what Theresa told me, I knew he had some health challenges of his own. I also knew that Emily's mom passed when she was young. Her father raised his daughters on his own after that. He deserved to come home to a quiet house if that's what he wanted. Both Theresa and Emily assured me he was fine with our visit, but so far, he was nowhere to be seen.

"Where's your dad, Em?" I asked.

"Oh, he's gone out for the night."

"Card game, bowling or book club?"

"No. None of those," she said and left it at that.

"I hope he didn't feel like he had to leave on our account."

"No. That's okay. He just needs his space sometimes."

Harrison cut in, "Can we have the cake now, Mommy? Can we have the cake? I want to show the kids the soccer on TV and eat the cake. Can we have the cake and watch the soccer?" Emily pulled a store-bought cake out of the fridge and we sliced it up for the kids.

After everyone was done eating, I helped cleanup the dishes while Theresa and Emily swapped stories about old classmates. The conversation returned to Emily's date and how a person in her forties goes about making such a connection online without feeling totally grossed out. I excused myself to do a much-needed load of laundry and check in with the kids.

Henry, Max and Harper were dragging. Their energy was no match for Harrison's. He was bouncing from toy trains to TV channels to repeated room tours all while my kids sat on the wrap-around couch looking stoned. I set up our sleeping bags in a side room and inflated an air mattress Emily lent us for Theresa and me to crash on. Then I told the kids to shower and get ready for bed. Harrison was not having it.

"It's not bedtime! It's not *my* bedtime!"

"Harrison, honey, they're tired," Emily explained from the other room.

"I'm not going to bed!" Then he sprinted upstairs. "It's not *my* bedtime!" A number of loud crashes followed as Emily rolled her eyes in exasperation and bounded up the stairs after him.

A few minutes later, she came down pulling a wet-faced Harrison by the hand.

While they were gone, I'd poked around the living room and found a few kid-friendly books tucked into corners and under couches. "Hey, Harrison," I said. "Harper's done with her shower. How about the three of us sit together here on the couch and I'll read these books to you guys."

"Okay," he said, but he didn't look too happy about it. "I'll sit with you if Harper sits too."

Some of my favorite times as a parent have been spent reading stories to my kids. I've read laying on the floor in the living room, from the passenger seat on long car drives to the lake, snuggled together with them on the couch, or rocking under a lamp — book on my lap — as they sat huddled up by my feet. I read the entire *Harry Potter* series to Henry and then again to Max. I was halfway through *The Goblet of Fire* with Harper; I brought it along on the trip and read it to her most nights. But before we arrived at Emily's, I told her we probably would need to take a night off from *Harry*; I didn't know if Harrison had heard any of the story before and I didn't want to spoil it for him by reading ahead.

I settled in with "The Lorax," "The Little Engine that Could," and some book about Thomas the Train (Thankfully, my kids never drank the Thomas Kool-Aid). "Read the Thomas book! Thomas! *Thomas!* Thomas!" Harrison pleaded.

"Okay, buddy. We'll start with that one." I began to read, but halfway through Harrison slipped off the couch and turned on the TV. "No TV while we're reading, pal, okay?"

"Harrison . . ." Emily pulled away from her conversation with Theresa in the kitchen. "Mr. Matt is trying to read, now you sit still and listen."

"Dad, I'm tired," Harper said. "Can I go to bed?"

"No! Read! *Read!* Read!" Harrison cried.

"HARR-is-SON! Don't make Mommy have to shout."

"Emily, it's cool, I got it," I said.

But I didn't have it. I like to think I'm pretty good with kids. I've got a whole set of made up stories I tell to the nieces and nephews when we get together with Theresa's side of the family. My nephew, Elijah, always tells me I should publish them. One of my favorite games to play with kids is to ask them to give me three things: a character, an object, and a place. Then I have to make up a story off the top of my head that includes all of them. Even these tricks didn't work with Harrison. Eventually, Emily had to take him upstairs.

"He's just really excited," she said, wiping sweat out of her eyes. "Sometimes he's a handful. But I love him." Again, that hollow laugh.

THERESA finished our load of laundry. When I went to get our kids settled, I found both Henry and Max already in their sleeping bags. I tucked Harper in and by the time I'd finished singing her two songs, she was sound asleep.

I set up the air mattress while Theresa and Emily talked for a while longer in the kitchen. I wanted to join them, but we had started the day in Santa Barbara, spent the better part of the afternoon in L.A. and the evening, as it was, in San Diego; I was worn out. Plus, I knew we'd be driving to Joshua Tree National Park tomorrow, a little more than four hours according to our route, I wanted to be sure to have my legs under me for the drive. I'm not sure when I fell asleep, but it was before Theresa came to bed.

I woke up to a sharp light coming from the front door. There was a backlit man standing in the doorway, clutching a bag in his right hand. He muttered to himself and banged something down on the front table. Still half-asleep, I tried to get up quickly, but the air mattress had lost half its loft. Kicking my legs in the air like a turtle on its back; I finally found enough purchase to roll myself onto the floor. "Who's there?!" I said.

"Matt! What the hell?" Theresa shout-whispered. "That's just Emily's dad!"

"Sorry. Sorry," I said. He mumbled something indistinguishable in reply and walked out of the room.

Theresa was suspended just a few inches off the ground, which gave my side of the air mattress the look of a hot air balloon lolling on its side in the process of being filled. I went to the bathroom, and when I came back I found the bed looking more stable and Harper lying in my place. I guess I'd woken her up with my mad scrambling.

"Daddy, can I sleep with Mommy?" she asked.

"Ask Mommy," I said. But Theresa was already snoring. "Okay. Fine. Yes."

The jolt of adrenaline I experienced because of the "break in" still simmered in my blood as I pulled my sleeping bag off of the melting mattress and settled down onto the floor. After a restless twenty minutes, I started to get pissed. It was too hot to sleep. A number of fans were set up to circulate the air, and they clicked and buzzed like an oscillating concert of crickets. The mattress breathed a slow, low hiss of once cushioning air out of its unidentified leak every time either Theresa or Harper rolled over. I was about to give up, go into the living room and watch some TV or something, when I suddenly thought of something that hadn't crossed my mind for a very long time.

Once when I was little, my brother and I spent the night at my Grandma Bindig's house while my parents were away on a rare adult-only trip. I woke up in the middle of the night and couldn't fall back asleep. I went to my Grandma's bedside and told her. She came back in with me to my room to tuck me in. After reading me another story she told me that, when she couldn't sleep, she liked to lay back and count her blessings. I remember being confused.

"Blessings?"

"Like you and your brother. And Grandpa. And your Dad and Mom. And all of your aunts and uncles. Your cousins. This house. And food. And the woods. And the creek."

I remember thinking, "Those aren't blessings. Those are just my life." But I didn't say that aloud and I'm glad I didn't. My Grandma would have been ashamed. I regret taking so much for granted as a kid. Now I know better.

So I whispered my blessings into the silence and present pain of Emily's sleeping house. It was another hour before I finally fell asleep.

AFTER a hearty breakfast together, we took a walk over to see Emily's school, just to stretch our legs ahead of the long drive. On the way back, I carried Harrison on my shoulders as he bounced up and down singing a Thomas the Train song. He hugged each of us when we got back to the house, "I will miss you! I will miss you! I will *miss* you!" he said, slapping the top of my head for emphasis.

"He's a sweet kid, Emily," I said. And after all he's been through, I meant it too.

SEVERAL years earlier, Theresa flew to San Diego to visit her friend, Ami, who was making a go of it out West. One of the highlights of her trip was a visit to Old Town, an encampment near the Mexican border where Theresa still swore she ate the best food she's ever had in her life. I mean a tortilla *cannot* be consumed in our house without Theresa saying something like, "This is pretty good, but this one time, when I went to Old Town, near San Diego . . . I'm not kidding, Matt . . . They just absolutely melted in your mouth." Such was the legend of this food that we made a point of driving out of our way to experience it for ourselves.

Old Town was fun in a falsely festive, exploitive, touristy kind of way. My bullshit meter kept buzzing, as I looked at all the industry folks in "ethnic" garb making their way through the crowds of tourists. But when Ed, our waiter came over, I started to lighten up. He told us he lives in San Diego, but drives down to Old Town for work everyday because it reminds him of when he was a kid. He showed us a trick with salt that helps fight off the tongue-on-fire feeling you get from Old Town food. And he slipped us an extra order of tortillas after I told him how obsessed Theresa is with them. Yeah, I liked the place much better after old Ed showed up. He was the real deal.

And Theresa was right about the food. It *was* very good. We ate lots and lots and lots of it and still managed to carry two take-out packages back to the car with us. Although the thought of ever eating again was about as attractive to me as the idea of trying to read the entire *Harry Potter* series to Harrison while simultaneously listening to the Thomas the Train theme song on endless repeat, we stuffed our leftovers into the cooler for later. Then for the first time, I steered the Sequoia away from the coast. We were headed for the desert.

Max, Henry and Harper — getting into the kitschy spirit. Old Town. San Diego, California.

WE hummed along past tawny expanses shimmering under wispy-white clouds in an impossibly blue sky. Rolling, rock-filled fields housed sun-soaked sheds and broken-down windmills rusting in the heat. Survivor shrubs, somehow still green, stretched their parched hopes toward the sky. We passed boulders piled house-high like marbles carelessly left on the floor of a playroom for the gods. The distant peaks looked like crayon-colored pages: the edges dark and bold stood out against a faded field of the same hues. It was 114 degrees outside when we glided through Palm Springs just before 5:00 p.m.. The inside of the Sequoia's windshield was too hot to touch.

By the time we pulled into The Twenty-nine Palms Inn, the sky was beginning to bruise. After checking into our room we decided, close as we were to the park, to take a drive inside to watch the nightfall.

I'd read about a place called Skull Rock, so we made our way there hoping for a quick climb before the sun set. We pulled up next to a short trail. From the road you could easily see where the rock got its name: a rounded dome, two clear empty sockets for eyes, a bent nose cavern and a sand-slashed mouth. As the kids clambered up the path, Theresa's warnings of snakes and falls ignored, I found my head full of memories of Henry's childhood obsession with the story of *Peter Pan*.

The Golden Book version of Barrie's tale was the first book Henry was able to read by himself. Disney's film version (even with its unacceptably racist depiction of the Indians) was the first full-length movie he ever watched.

I made him a complete costume out of green felt and he used to creep in it on the couch-top, clutching the small wooden sword we made together at my basement workbench, pretending to be

Peter Pan looking for his lost shadow. "Are you Peter Pan?" I asked him.

"No," he countered dramatically. "I'm a dark figgurr."

Before Harper was born, we took the boys to see a theatrical version of the story put on at a small playhouse in Buffalo. The actor who played Mr. Darling — Wendy's imagination-starved father — also played Captain Hook. The implication didn't escape my notice. An adulthood such as Mr. Darling's, devoid of imagination, adventure, and fun is synonymous with evil. It's the true and worthy opponent, lurking on the other side of adolescence. Waiting for us all.

Henry is thirteen now. Done with Peter Pan. Old enough to listen to rap, snapchat with friends, and fearlessly lead his siblings up a fissure in the side of Skull Rock, looking for a better view of the star-strewn sky. "Come on, Mom and Dad!" he called down to us. "Come up!"

"Come up! Come up!" Harper and Max shouted at us like a pair of Lost Boys.

"We should go," I said.

"You go," Theresa replied. "I'll stay. One of us has to call 9-1-1."

"Come on, Dad!" Henry called down again. "It's not *hard*. You can do it!"

"I know I *can* do it, boy!" I shouted back, a sudden anger rising. The smile on Henry's face dropped a little. I guess he wasn't calling me out. He just wanted to play.

"Stay still. I'll be right up," I said.

"Don't worry, Dad. We'll wait for you."

But kids don't wait. There is no Neverland. They grow. They climb. They read stories by themselves that you used to read together and then, just as suddenly, they don't read those stories anymore at all.

I panted onto the top of Skull Rock and stood with my children looking out as the night sky spread across the dome of the desert "Look, there's the Big Dipper." Henry said. I nodded in agreement. But I wasn't looking for constellations. Against all probability, I was looking for the second star to the right.

Tear Down the Walls
(Day 6. Joshua Tree — The Grand Canyon)

THE ONLY PLACE IN the world where you can find Joshua Trees, scientifically known as Yucca Brevifolia, is the Mojave Desert. Legend has it when Mormon settlers first spotted the trees with their shaggy bark, twisted, up-reaching branches and ball-like clusters of pointed leaves sticking out at all angles, they dubbed them Joshua Trees in a nod to Moses's buddy, Joshua, from the Old Testament. The legend gets fuzzy after that (as legends do) as to *which* part of the Joshua/Moses story the Mormons were thinking of when they came up with the catchy moniker, but regardless, the name stuck.

The first time I heard about Joshua Trees of course wasn't in The Book of Mormon, or the Old Testament, but rather when I was in fifth grade and U2 released their iconic album, *The Joshua Tree* featuring hits like, "Where the Streets Have No Name," "I Still Haven't Found What I'm Looking For," and "With or Without You." Plus it has an epically cool album cover: Adam Clayton, Larry Mullen Jr. and The Edge all dressed in black and staring straight at you, while Bono, the prophet of the bunch, looks off to the left at a range of lonely desert mountains behind him. What better setting for exploring the soul than a desert?

Henry — standing in the shadow of a Joshua Tree.
Joshua Tree National Park.

THE alarm woke us up before the sun, and we sleepily ate snacks sitting cross-legged on the floor of our room in the Twenty-nine Palms Inn before pulling out for the park. It was just after 6:00 a.m.. I cued up *The Joshua Tree* as we drove past the sign outside the ranger station greeting visitors with the comforting welcome,

"Do Not Die Today," followed by a list of precautions to take to avoid untimely demise: *If your shadow is shorter than you, seek shade. Tell a friend where you are going. Avoid hiking 11 a.m.-6 p.m.*

When Theresa and I told people our plans to hike in the Mojave Desert in August with our seven, ten and thirteen year-olds, all of them warned us to "watch out for the dry heat." Dry heat? What does that mean? Back in Buffalo when it's 90 degrees in the summer, it can feel like you're trying to breathe in a bowl of soup when you walk out to get the mail. But it's not like that in the desert. Have you ever turned a hair dryer on full blast and pointed it directly at your face? That's dry heat. It made my nostrils feel weird.

We parked the Sequoia by the side of the road and headed down a trail toward a place just past Skull Rock called The Hidden Valley. The sun filled the sky with light at an alarming rate, and any coolness that clung to morning was quickly burnt away. Our map claimed the trail was a two-mile loop, which seemed a manageable distance for us even if the heat got crazy, but it turns out the "trail" was really more like a slightly worn path, not marked in any obvious way.

Because I'm a teacher and a storyteller, people often assume I'm most comfortable in a crowd with all of the attention on me, but the truth is I really like being alone. Let me put it this way, I've gone to professional football games by myself before, sitting alone with my nachos, while groups of crazies on either side of me slapped backs and chatted with each other over the din of the game, totally ignoring me in the process — and I totally enjoyed myself. Like, really had a good time. But there's a big difference between being "alone" in a football stadium full of people and being *alone* in the desert.

A deluminator is a magical instrument invented by the great

wizard, Albus Dumbledore from the *Harry Potter* series. The way it works is you point it at a light source (street lamp, night light, chandelier) and click its button. The light you're pointing at gets sucked into the deluminator and the user is left in total darkness. Very useful when trying to be sneaky.

Imagine an alternative version of the deluminator — call it the denoiser. Instead of sucking the light out of a scene, it sucks out the sound. That's what the Mojave Desert was like that morning. No low hum of the heater. No cars driving by out front. No clicks, pops and whistles coming from the headphones of some guy on the street. All available noise evaporated in the wind — even the crunching of stones beneath our feet — the usual soundtrack of our hikes together. It was a little scary.

It's weird. In the desert, distance, like sound, is distorted. You see a stand of Joshua Trees ahead and think, "Oh, cool. We'll be there in a second." But five minutes later you're still walking toward it. Everything feels both close *and* far away.

It was approaching 100 degrees by the time we climbed back into the Sequoia. I wasn't sweaty at all, but my shirt was stained with salt at the neck and pits. Dry heat.

When we got back to the inn, Theresa and I packed up while the kids swam in the pool. We jumped in too when everything was in its place in the car, laughing at how quickly our skin dried after sitting in the sun

After we ate breakfast, I asked for access to the kitchen so I could fill up the extra eight water jugs I brought for the trip across the desert. It's the old Boy Scout in me. You know, "Be prepared." I didn't want to break down on the road without water.

Out there, the ground is always hot, no matter how deep they dig, so the water comes out of the tap *warm*. The only way you can make it cold is to load it with ice. But I skipped the ice, filled the jugs in the kitchen and took them out to the car.

Before we left, I visited the office to check out. When we checked in, I noticed a small lending library in the corner of the room. Maybe someone would want to read while sitting by the pool. So I gave the woman behind the desk a signed copy of my novel (I packed a bunch of them for just this purpose). "How much do I owe you?" she asked.

"Free of charge," I said. "It makes me feel good just to know my story's out there."

MAYBE this is what freedom is really all about. Not fireworks on the Fourth of July, apple pie, and you and your neighbor flying different flags for whichever set of lives you think matters. Not any of that shit. Maybe freedom is a desert at sunrise — vast and open with no clear path. Sure, it's a little disorienting. You can't really tell whether or not you're getting anywhere. You've just gotta keep going. Hoping against hope. Trusting that between your resources and your wit, you'll make it through before the land claims you for its own.

I cranked the music up high as we set our sights, once again, for the open road.

> *I want to run.*
>
> *I want to hide.*
>
> *I want to tear down the walls that hold me inside.*
>
> *I want to reach out, and touch the flame.*
>
> *Where the streets have no name.*

THERE'S a fine line between fear and excitement, and I crossed it somewhere along Route 40 between Joshua Tree and the Grand Canyon. There were stretches, (I'm talking thirty minute stretches), where there was literally no other car in sight.

My mind started peeking into dark places.

What if someone got suddenly sick? Over my thirteen years as a parent, I've been barfed on enough to know that's possible. Anytime. Anywhere.

And what if we got into an accident? Okay, that didn't seem very likely; usually you don't get into an accident unless there are other cars around. But, what if the Sequoia broke down? The check engine light turned on when we were leaving Emily's only to switch off a while later. It hadn't turned on again since we left Old Town, but still. We read in the owner's manual that the light sometimes turns on after passing certain mileage points, just so you'll take it in for a maintenance check. The odometer passed 30,000 just before Joshua Tree. But what if it was something more. Would eight gallons of water be enough to hold us over in the 100-degree heat?

We were miles and miles from anywhere and anyone. The truth was if something happened, it would be up to us to figure out how to make it through. It would be up to *me*.

Jesus, I thought, I'm just a *boy*. Why do I have all these responsibilities? Then reality shifted again into gear. I'm in my mid-forties. I have a twenty-year career going. I've got a mortgage, life insurance, and a goddamn will. I'm the guy in charge now. There is no cavalry.

I've got a picture hanging in my classroom with Emerson's famous quote written on it. "What lies behind us and what lies before us are tiny matters compared to what lies within us." I've always loved that quote, but just then I looked in the rearview:

nothing behind us. Then I looked up ahead: nothing before us either. Just the road and the desert.

What if what's within me isn't good enough?

"Let's listen to some music," Theresa said. She grabbed my phone and opened the music app. "Who do you want to listen to?"

"You choose."

"Can we listen to "Old Town Road"? Max shouted from the back.

"No. How about The Beatles, The White Album?"

Theresa nodded and swiped up on the phone until she found the icon for the album. Then she pushed play, leaned her seat back and put her feet up on the dash.

All the chatter in the car ceased as we listened from "Back in the U.S.S.R." all the way through "Good Night." By the time the music stopped we were out of the desert, into Arizona and heading due north toward the Grand Canyon. Thank God for The Beatles.

WE arrived at the Ten X campground — a mile or so outside of Grand Canyon National Park — just after four o'clock. I had the boys help me set up the tent while Theresa and Harper scoped out the bathroom and water situation; there was a pump down a path about 100 yards from our site and the bathrooms weren't far either.

We hung the hammock and gathered some wood to chop for the fire. We were in the process of setting up the sleeping bags when we heard a small voice from behind the parked Sequoia. "Hello? Futbol?" A small boy pointed a furtive finger three sites away to where a large motorhome was parked next to an electric hookup. There was a group of adults and children playing a haphazard game of soccer in the open space next to the vehicle. I looked over and, thanks to two semesters of required language work in college, quickly recognized the snippets of the game chatter I heard as French.

"Oui, oui," I said. My children looked at me like I was crazy. "He wants you guys to join the game over there," I said.

"Okay! Sure. Can we?" Max said.

"We're going to eat dinner soon and then head to the park, but you can play for a little bit if you want."

"Yeah?" the French boy asked. My boys nodded their heads and started to follow. But after a few steps the French boy stopped and said, "La jeune fille?" and pointed at Harper. "Your . . . young . . . girl?"

"Harper, do you want to go too?" Without another word, she pulled on her sneakers and took off toward the game. "Keep an eye on her, Henry. We'll be right here."

Theresa and I finished prepping camp and got everything set for bedtime so that if we got back late from sunset at the Canyon, we wouldn't have too much work to do before we settled in. Then we finished dishing up the freeze-dried meals.

The whole time we worked together we kept stealing glances over at the soccer game. It was a buzz of action: at least two sets of parents and six or seven kids, not counting our three. Eventually I walked over and waved the kids back for dinner. "Merci!" I cried to the French dad who seemed to be leading the effort.

"Bien sur!" he shouted back without looking up from the game.

Freeze-dried meals are an acquired taste, but we were hungry and choked them down okay. When we finished eating I walked with Henry to the water pump to do the dishes.

"So, Dad, you speak a little French, huh?"

"Yeah, un peu," I said, holding up my pointer finger and thumb an inch apart in front of my face.

"How do you say, 'Hi, I'm Henry. What's your name?'"

"Bonjour, je m'appelle Henry, comment t'appelles-tu?"

"Uh . . . okay."

"Why? Do you want to say hello to someone over there or something?"

"Not hello. I just want to know her name."

"*Her* name, huh?"

"Dad, don't be like that."

"Well, practice: 'Bonjour, je m'appelle Henry, comment t'appelles-tu?' Actually you should probably say 'Salut' instead of 'Bonjour'. 'Salut" is less formal." We were walking back to the campsite. Henry was holding the dishpan and soap. I cradled the clean dishes in my arms.

"Salut," Henry said. "What was the rest of it?"

"Salut, je m'appelle Henry, comment t'appelles-tu?'

"Salut," he said again, but before he could say more a young girl's voice answered.

"Salut!" She was coming from the bathrooms just behind us on her way back to the camper. She must have overheard Henry. Henry and I stood facing her. Like him, she still was slightly sweaty from the game, but her hair was long, her eyes were dark and her smile glowed. I could tell why he wanted to talk to her, but my boy said nothing.

I jumped in, "Salut. J'ai etudie le francaise pour quatre ans a l'ecole. Je m'appelle, Matt."

"What did you say to her, Dad?"

"I told her I studied French in school and that my name's Matt."

"Oh. My. God," Henry's cheeks burned scarlet.

"Qui est-ce?" the French girl asked, pointing at Henry and breaking into a little laugh.

"He's Henry," I said.

"Henry," she said.

"Je m'appelle . . . your name?" Henry asked her.

"Marie," the French girl said. "I am, Marie. We . . . are . . . traveling," she said in halting English.

"We are also traveling," Henry said. They both stood there looking at the ground in silence.

Having mostly exhausted my French and wanting to get to the Canyon before the sunset, I said, "Marie, we have to go. Au revoir."

"Au revoir," she said to me. Then she looked at Henry again, "Au revoir, Henry."

"Okay. Bye."

After a few steps I slapped him on the back and said, "Nice job, bud."

"Dad! Oh my God!" was all he could muster in reply.

Clouds were rolling in, obscuring the sun in its descent, as we parked the Sequoia and headed up the paved walkway toward Mather Point. I was just about jogging. I couldn't believe after everything, all the planning, the shopping, the packing and driving, we were finally here.

As our family gathered at an open spot on the railing along the rim my breath squeezed out of me. I couldn't speak. Tears welled in my eyes and spilled down my cheeks. As if on cue, the sky melted from slate blue thunderheads to a citrus shine, boomeranging back to earth and painting the canyon walls with a myriad of colorful streaks drawn by the strokes of God's fingers.

Then I was the little boy scraping barnacles off of a conch shell on a Cape Cod morning, sunburnt shoulders, blonde curls over my eyes.

I was on the side of the bathtub, talking to my brother as he slammed his finger in his throat over and over again, sobbing nonsense between gags as my parents raced around the house waiting for the ambulance to arrive.

I was in a pile of bodies, my right pinkie turned horribly crooked at the joint, wedged in the facemask of the St. Lawrence ball carrier. But there was no pain; just joy. It was fourth and one, and now it was over; we won.

And Theresa and I were again in my Pontiac Sunbird on our way to Niagara Falls. I convinced her to go against all logic, "Ride with me." Two hours there, two hours back. "Sure, we'll get back late, but who cares? Class doesn't start until after nine tomorrow morning." She'd never been there before. We talked the whole way, listening to mixtapes and laughing at each other's stories. It was sleeting, icy and cold. I found a parking spot close to the path and walked with her through the lingering Christmas lights to the brink of the falls. The roar of the water as it pounded over the rocks in the night made us talk louder than the moment called for. You're not supposed to yell at church.

And that was all of it. First a kiss in the dark, now the Grand Canyon with our kids. I'm telling you, man. All of it was *right there*.

The Whole Truth
(Day 7. The Grand Canyon)

WHEN I WAS FOUR years old, my father took my seven-year-old brother and me to see the re-release of *Star Wars*, which would eventually be re-named, *A New Hope*. On the way home, we stopped at *Brand Names*, a store that carried everything from weed whackers to banana-seat bicycles, where my father bought us our first "Star Wars guys." In a sure sign of things to come, I picked out the hero, Luke Skywalker (complete with a sliding lightsaber built into his arm), and my brother selected Darth Vader. Even as a little kid, I knew that money was pretty tight in our house. Going to the movies was a rare thing. Getting a new toy on top of that made it feel like Christmas.

One of my first vivid memories is running down a narrow strip of driveway between my parents' orange Volkswagen Beetle and our little house, and accidentally sanding off some of Luke Sky-walker's painted-on hair by rubbing his head against the rough brick. I remember looking down at the newly formed bald spot on the top of my hero's head and feeling, maybe for the first time in my life, a deep sense of regret at my carelessness. No one wants a bald, budding Jedi. When I showed my father what I'd done and asked him to "fix it," he laughed and told me something I'll never forget: "Some things just can't be undone, buddy."

WE'VE made a point of keeping violent first person video games out of our house, and when the kids were really little, we did our best to minimize their exposure to shoot 'em up movies too. That said, if you had told new-dad-me, in a few years time I'd be sitting with nine year-old Henry and six-year-old Max in a packed opening-weekend theater getting ready to watch the appropriately PG-13 rated, *The Force Awakens* — a movie that opens with a masked marauder ruthlessly slaughtering a village of innocents, I'd have said it was just as likely as me handing each of my kids a glass of paint thinner and daring them to take a sip. It's funny what we talk ourselves into as parents just because *our parents* did a similar thing. Yet there I was, holding Max's sweaty little hand as Henry dug what was left of his bitten-down fingernails into my other forearm, watching together as Kylo Ren stalked his father, Han Solo, with death in his eyes.

Max, who once spent the better part of *three hours* on a car trip repeatedly flipping a penny, and alternately a nickel, in the air so he could determine which coin was more likely to land face up, was screwing himself lower and lower into his seat and watching the action through open slits in his pudgy fingers. As the scene came to its climax and Solo and Ren faced off on a catwalk, I heard Max muttering to himself, "The good guys always win! The good guys always win!" and my heart simply broke.

"Oh, my sweet little boy," I wanted to tell him, "no they don't. They don't. Even when you think that this time they *really* should." I wanted to scoop him up, take him out of that darkened theater and buy him a chocolate milkshake. Then I'd take him to the park, where we'd sit, criss cross applesauce on a blanket in the shade of a sycamore tree. And I'd safely explain, using all of the right words, that the arc of the moral universe may indeed bend toward justice, but the length of that curve is long and slow. And chances are he may never see its end. Han Solo may be the hero we love, but a lot of the time it's the bad guy in black who wins the day. But how do you say that to a six-year old?

Well, maybe you can't. Maybe they haven't invented those kinds of words yet. Maybe, instead, you just have to take them to movies and hold their hand. And when they ask you later, tell them that, yes, sometimes it does end like that. The bad guys win. I'm sorry to say. That's the truth, buddy. But it isn't the *whole* truth. I promise. It's way more complicated than that.

I woke up at the first sign of light and dressed quietly so as not to disturb everyone before grabbing my journal and unzipping myself out of the tent and into the air of the morning. Truth be told, I wanted a few minutes to myself. The swirl of emotions I felt visiting the Canyon the night before was too much to take in at the time. I needed to dream on them, and now, make sense of them in my journal before they got lost in the wash of our day's activities.

I wish I were a more disciplined writer, who made time every day to hone my craft. That's what all the writing books tell you to do, anyway. But as a parent/teacher/writer I've found that's unrealistic bullshit. Which is why I stopped reading those stupid "how-to" writing books a long time ago. Besides if I have free time to spend, why would I spend it reading about writing instead of *actually writing*? It's like reading a book about sex. I mean, figuring it out is the fun part, right? Just get going. But just as nobody I know has as much sex as they want to, I guess it's also probably safe to say that no father-of-young-children-who-also-juggles-a-couple-of-jobs-to-help-make-ends-meet writer has as much time to write as he'd like to either. Point is you've got to get it while you can. Even if that means waking up before dawn in a campground outside of the Grand Canyon and sitting on a still-dewy picnic bench to chase a few paragraphs onto the page before breakfast.

The stillness of the morning lent itself to reflection. I wrote uninterrupted. The only sound was my breath and the pen scratching across the page. Eventually though, and this has happened to me a few other times when I've been writing, I began to feel the presence of some "other" there in the campground with me. I'm not above believing in mystical shit, especially when I'm sitting just over a mile away from the Grand Canyon, so I thanked the spirit for its presence and turned to the next blank page. Then I heard a twig snap.

Standing a shadow's width away, with its head dipped into the scrub grass under the ponderosa pines, was a bulky bull elk. His full rack of antlers lolled from side to side as he munched his morning meal. I read about these elk. Not native to Arizona, they were brought to the state by hunters seeking game. Now, with human sprawl dwindling their natural predators, the elk population has exploded in problematic ways, leading to dangerous encounters (a full grown male elk can weigh up to 800 pounds) with people dumb enough to try to snap selfies with a wild animal. Of course, none of this came to mind that morning. Instead, fully taken by the presence of the beast, I sat in stillness taking the elk's proximity as a gift from the writing gods.

Slowly he strode away from our campsite toward a larger clump of grass, and with the wonder still wet on the canvas of my mind, I turned again to the pages of my journal, trying impossibly to capture the magic of the moment. When I looked up again, the elk was gone and standing in his place was Max rubbing the sleep out of his eyes.

"I had to pee," he said. "What are you doing?"

"Writing."

"What are you writing about?" he asked. Then I told him about the elk.

"He just walked up to the table," I said. "Just like he was looking for breakfast. He was standing right where you're standing, Max." Max turned on his spot as if looking for a hatch into which the elk might have escaped. "Wait, it wasn't you was it?" I asked. "You're not a shape-shifter or something are you? All these years pretending to be just my regular middle child when in reality you're really an elk?"

"No," Max said, still sleepy, but smiling at my joke anyway. Then his eyes shot bright and his body turned rigid. "There he is!" Max stage whispered. "He's back."

He was further away than he had been when I first caught sight of him, but it was him all right, back again, with his eyes trained on the ground, his mouth busy with the grass. "Can I go see him," Max asked.

"He's a wild animal, Max. You can see him from here."

"No, but, Dad, just a little closer?"

"A little closer is all," I said. "But not too close." This is the kind of thing that drives Theresa crazy. More than once she's claimed that my years of battling 300-pound behemoths as an under-sized nose guard has given me an over-inflated sense of my own ability to wrestle my way out of tough situations.

This is *perhaps* true.

But while I *may* have overestimated my ass-kicking ability once or twice before, it's not like I was doing ass-kicking (or should

I say, elk-kicking) calculus here. I wasn't sitting there thinking, "Okay, if this 800 pound creature charges my nine-year old son, I'll just leg-whip the fucker and everything'll be fine." I'm not an idiot. But I don't know, maybe the dreamlike stillness of the morning or the mist that clung like clouds to the spindly upper branches of the pines was affecting me. Either way, I just didn't *feel* any sort of danger. The vibes were all good. "Just not too close," I said again. Then I turned back to my journal, trusting that Max would know when to stop.

I should say now that Max has a sort of *thing* for wild creatures. Once while walking down a busy street in New York City we almost lost him to a car's bumper because he was chasing a pigeon, sure that if he focused enough he would be able to grab it before it took flight. He sometimes sits like Buddha on the ground under our bird feeder with handfuls of seeds on his knees hoping to lure chipmunks into his grasp. One of my favorite pictures is of him holding a frog he caught and kissed.

When I finished writing the last page of the morning, I looked up to find that both Max and the elk were gone.

It's amazing what a surge of adrenaline can do to your mind. At once I saw again a page of the National Park website I must have encountered while researching the trip which recommended a "safe viewing distance" of 100 feet (or, as they said, two bus-lengths) when encountering elk along the South Rim. Knowing that sudden movements and unexpected sounds can startle even the most docile of creatures into hostile action, I resisted my temptation to shout Max's name and sprint toward the spot where I'd last seen the elk, and instead placed my journal on the table and began walking as softly as I could around the edge of our campsite and into the thicker stands of trees.

When I came upon him, Max was standing inches away from the elk with a tuft of grass in his hand.

"Max!" I whispered. "What are you doing?!" He put his finger to his lips in response and lifted his hand to the elk's now raised snout. In one swift movement the elk took the grass from Max's hand then turned its attention back to ground. Max turned to look at me as if to ask for direction, but I was frozen to the spot.

Then, with the measured motions of a person who had done this sort of thing a thousand times before, Max reached his hand out and placed it softly on the elk's head — his wide stretched thumb and pinky finger touching each of the antlers.

At this the elk raised himself to his full height. And looked Max, who had not yet removed his hand from the elk's head, square in the eyes.

"Max!" I whispered once again, horrified that I was about to see my child gored. But when he turned to look at me, the expression on his face was so full of wonder, his eyes so full of light, that I swear I was looking at his spirit rather than his human form. My breath caught and my eyes watered. Goosebumps shot over my arms and legs. My spine danced with nerves. The elk slowly rolled his head from side to side, as Max dance-dodged the antlers, the creature's face inches from his own.

Then, at once the elk was a stone statue. Tall. Rigid. His eyes wide. His ears alert. I saw in this new posture an emotion that henceforth had been a stranger to the morning: fear.

"Max! Come away!" I said, no longer bothering to whisper. "Now!"

Max lifted his hand as the elk raised its nose into the air and let out a quick snort. A shot of urine splashed the floor of the forest. I waved my hand quickly, beckoning my son toward me. Without hesitation, quickly now, Max walked backward away from the elk; lifting his feet as if out of buckets, his eyes fixed on the beast in front of him until he was close enough for me to grab his shoulders. We looked at each other in shared awe, our mouths open in astonished smiles, and then turned our eyes back to the elk. He was already walking away.

A Roosevelt Elk. Mature males weigh between 700-1,200 lbs. Ten X Campground, Kaibab National Forest. Grand Canyon Village, Arizona.

THERESA was pretty quiet as Max and I recounted the story of the elk. I expected an earful from her. Why hadn't I intervened? Didn't I know that Max could have been killed? But if she had those thoughts, she kept them to herself — even after the kids went off to fill up our water bladders at the camp's pumping station.

We washed up the dishes together, packed our daypacks, and settled the camp as best as we could. With all the "have tos" done, and the kids occupied with getting themselves ready, we sat down together to eat, alone and unoccupied for the first time since we left home a week ago.

All the marriage counselors tell you that if you hope to survive as a couple, you've got to "make time" for each other: date nights, a weekend away at a trendy bed and breakfast, a candlelit bedroom with a jar of massage oil waiting for her after she's finished putting the kids to bed. What's funny is these same folks tell you you've *also* got to "make time" for yourself: develop a side hobby, pursue a fitness goal, regularly meet up with a core group of friends, or take an online class. Whatever. And I get what they mean: you need to prioritize the things that actually matter: your wife, your soul — over the less important bullshit that otherwise occupies your time: the sticky spot on the bathroom floor next to the toilet, the pile of papers that should have been graded a week ago. It's an objective fact that this woman you're going through life with is more important than dried piss, but all the same, time isn't something you "make" unless you're God. Like our capacity to pay attention, there are limits when it comes to time.

For just one moment though, there in the cool Arizona morning, with a day at the Canyon on our minds, Theresa and I sat across from each other sipping our coffee and tea, our feet twisted together on the pine needle-strewn forest floor, tin bowls of instant oatmeal steaming in our laps. It was perfect.

BEFORE reading a particular book, some English teachers I know spend weeks with their class prepping their students for what is to come. If the class will be reading *The Great Gatsby* for instance, these teachers design mini-research projects to help their students learn all there is to learn about the Roaring Twenties and Fitzgerald's checkered personal life. Shoot, maybe they'll even read a piece or two of literary criticism about the book itself: What does the novel have to say about money, power and love? What claims does Fitzgerald make about who ought to be granted access to the American Dream? You get the idea. It's only after their students are prepped and prepared to properly fill in the blanks of meaning as they read along that these teachers allow their students to actually begin to read *Gatsby*.

Other teachers I know toss all of that over their shoulders. They hand their kids the book and dig in, sifting through the story and making meaning out of the class's collective response. This second breed of teacher lets the kids take the lead. To them, learning is about the process. They aren't overly concerned about whether or not they "cover" and "contextualize" the book. They prioritize a reader's response over learning "what the book is all about."

Kids who are taught in the first way walk away from reading a particular book with lots of canned knowledge. Come the end of the year, they'll do better on text-specific essay questions because they can dazzle the graders with the depth of their text-specific knowledge. Kids who are taught in the second way don't score as well on those kinds of questions, but they're usually more equipped when asked to make sense of a fresh text on their own because that's what they've been doing all along.

Which approach you take as a teacher really depends on what you're after. What's the point of reading books in school? Is it to give kids a deep and acute understanding of a handful of selected books and authors? Or is it to give them the tools they need to read the world around them with open eyes? Over the course of my twenty-plus year teaching career, I've thought a ton about the pros and cons of both of the above stated approaches and found that, like most things in life, balance is key.

I was thinking about all of this teaching shit as I stood pretending to contemplate which muffin to buy at the Mather Point Café. I admit that this is sort of tragic. I mean, here I was, on an epic family vacation — in *August* — and I was thinking about my fucking *job*. I guess Carl Jung was right: "You are what you do." But it wasn't like I just randomly started thinking about pedagogy. The train of thought happened for a reason.

See, while we were waiting for the bikes we rented from Bright Angel Bike Tours to get pulled around front so they could be properly fitted to each of us, Theresa took the kids to the National Park visitor center where they each procured pamphlets packed with prompts, stickers and tasks that, if properly followed, affixed and completed, would lead my children to be anointed "Junior Rangers," an honor that carries with it the benefit of a plastic replica ranger badge.

On one hand the Junior Ranger program seems like a good way to make a visit to the National Park an "educational experience" where kids get all they're supposed to get out of their day. On the other hand, the program seems like not only a thinly veiled effort to encourage foot traffic through some of the buildings near the rim, but also a ploy to keep kids busy and entertained. As if being at *The Grand Canyon* is not enough, kids have to chase after a plastic badge in order for the day to be deemed a success.

THE route of our ride took us on a paved path that sloped gently downward. The boys and our tour guide, Troy, chatting happily about God knows what, rode as much as a football field in front of Theresa, Harper and me who rolled along behind at a seven-year-old pace. The Canyon was always in full view, but very rarely were we close enough to the edge of it to feel any sort of rational danger. Not that that stopped movie scenes of Max flying over the handlebars as he crashed into the knee-high stone wall that rims the Canyon from playing on near constant repeat in my brain. I was a sheep dog circling my flock, constantly alert to every dangerous aspect of my surroundings. Fooling myself into believing that I could stop the worst from happening if I only stayed a step ahead.

But in my hyper-aware vigilance, I road-blocked a recognition of something sacred. Looking back, I see it now. "Here we are, Theresa," I should have said. "You and me. We've known each other since we were kids (Theresa was just 18 when we met and I was 21). We lost two of our children before they were born, argued about organic carpeting, and once drove twelve hours in a snowstorm to make it back home for Christmas. And now we are gliding on bikes with our three children next to one of the most amazing things a human being can experience. Here we are, Theresa. You and me."

A marriage is made up of so many of these moments, but what I've found is that most of the time, you're so busy worrying about staying in the trip budget, how much sunscreen to apply, or whether or not the snacks you've packed are both sufficiently healthy and palatable enough to please the three very different hungers you're hoping to keep at bay, that you seldom squeeze hands long enough to say I love you in the way such moments merit.

TROY skidded to stops and called us over several times on our journey from Hopi Point to Hermit's Rest. He pointed out plants, called our attention to creatures, told us tales, and answered our questions with such unrelenting friendliness that I couldn't help believing every single word he said.

Take, for example, the story he told us about a small black speck we saw miles away on the Canyon wall at one of our stops. "That speck is actually a cave, you guys," Troy said. "You could drive a minivan into it. A few years back, some scientist repelled down, just to check it out, and found fossilized bones of some ancient breed of buffalo. They figured the cave used to be the home to a prehistoric bird of prey who must have brought the buffalo home for dinner one night. Pretty crazy, right?"

His story-telling timing was great. Whenever a shadow of doubt started creeping across my face or my very sensitive bullshit meter began to buzz, he'd do something to pull me back in. Like the time he pointed down to the smudged blue line that is the Colorado River seen from the height of the Canyon's rim and said, "That ribbon of blue is why we're here. Before they dammed up the river starting way back in the early 1900s, that water down there cut through this country like a hot knife through butter. Forty-pound boulders as big as basketballs were pushed past points at a rate of eighty rocks per minute. That's enough to carve a canyon. Truth is this whole thing," he swept his hand across the broad swath of the horizon, "used to be under water." Then he nodded, and lowered his voice almost as if he was talking to himself. "Maybe it will be again some day?" A smile cracked his lips. Then he swung himself back onto his bike's saddle and began to peddle to the next stop. He didn't look back to make sure we were following him, but follow him we did.

THOUGH the morning ride was leisurely, by the time it was over the sun was fully up and the heat quickly sapped us of our energy. We found shelter and refueled at a cafeteria-style eatery on the grounds where we ordered up the kind of crappy, over-priced tourist food we had successfully avoided for most of the trip. After lunch Theresa helped the kids reorganize their bags and I went to the water station to refill our water bladders. Once the heat of the day passed, we hopped on a shuttle headed for the start of the Bright Angel Trail.

The Bindig family — riding Bright Angel Bicycles. South Rim, somewhere between Hopi Point and Hermit's Rest. Grand Canyon, Arizona

BEFORE we left for the trip, my friend Mike told me a story about trying to walk with his family down into the Canyon. "There are *no rails!*" he said. "They just carved out this little scab of a trail along the cliff edge. Like any second you could step off and plunge to your death!" I listened both trying to receive his words as a caring warning and doing my best to refuse to let them sink in. We didn't come to The Grand Canyon to look at it from the safe distance of the rim trail, we wanted in. "And for God's sake," Mike added, "If you guys are crazy enough to try it — did I mention we turned around after a few hundred yards? — If you're crazy enough to try it, *please* promise me you'll hold Max's hand the *entire* time." Max, who was with me and avidly listening as my friend tried to warn us away from one of our trip's signature moments, spoke up.

"How come he has to hold *my* hand?" Max asked.

"Because you could *die* if you fell, Max!" Mike shouted. "And you like to climb things, remember?"

As we drove away from Mike's house that day I looked in the rearview mirror at Max who was gazing out the window with a stoic look of contemplation on his face.

"Coach Mike didn't scare you, did he, buddy?" I asked.

"No, I'm not scared," Max said. "Besides falling into The Grand Canyon would be a cool way to die, you know."

"Maybe," I said. "But how about we don't try to find out this time around?"

THE trail was hot, as in early-August-in-Arizona hot, dusty, and very steep. We took it slow. Walking with an understanding that for every step we took down there would be two harder steps to take on our way back up. Begin with the end in mind, they say.

We had been hiking for an hour when we decided to stop to rest in the shade of a switchback bend on the Bright Angel Trail. Our hats were rimmed with sweat, our water bladders half empty and our socks covered in dust. Having just passed through the first of several tunnels dug into the cliffside on the eight-mile path down to the canyon floor, we rested among a cluster of car-sized rocks along the side of the trail. According to the map, we hadn't even covered a mile.

We turned our attention to our snacks, and were sitting in silence with our backs against the canyon wall when I noticed a man in black, about two hundred yards away, making his way toward us from the canyon floor with the river at his back.

I had just taken a deep bite of my second Clif bar when the man in black rounded the corner and came into clear view. Drenched in sweat, heaving heavy breaths, and climbing with the slanted gait of a man fighting against an unyielding gale, he approached us blindly and appeared to stagger slightly toward the edge of the trail.

"Hey friend," I said. "You look like you've come a long way today." He nodded and gulped at his water bottle. There was something in his eyes that gave me pause. "Do you want this?" I held up my half eaten Clif Bar. Without hesitation he took it from me, peeled off the wrapper and began to eat it as if it were the last morsel of food on planet Earth. My kids, who usually insist I pour my spare water into their mouths rather than drinking directly from my cup, looked on aghast: here was a *total stranger* eating the remains of my Cliff Bar!

"Thanks," he said, with sweat oozing into his eyes from his soaked hat. "I've been walking all day."

"Eight miles, bottom to top, right?"

"How much further do I have?" he asked.

"I'd guess a little under a mile." He sat down on a rock and looked out over the expansive view.

"I'm from Florida," he said. "Different kind of heat over here. Still hot though. Too hot to look while you're walking. Good to stop." His breathing worried me.

"Do you have enough water?"

He shook his head. "Almost out." I undid my backpack and slid the stopper across the top of my half-filled water bladder. Then I motioned for his water bottle, which he passed wordlessly to me. I filled it to the top then passed it back.

"You guys from Buffalo?" he asked. "I see the hats." He pointed to the Buffalo Bills bucket hats both of my boys were wearing. Henry nodded wordlessly. Max wriggled out of my grasp (as promised, I hadn't let go of his hand since we started down the trail) and pulled his hat from his head. He looked at the logo in the blinding sun for a second before nodding back at the stranger in recognition.

"How about you?" I asked. "You go for the Dolphins?"

"When I'm not doing things like this, hiking this damn trail in one day, I like to watch football."

"This is better than football," I said.

"When you stop it feels better. The climb is tough though. Like I said. I've been walking all day."

"Did you sleep down there last night then?" I nodded over my shoulder toward the dusty blue line of The Colorado.

"No. I walked down this morning. Now I'm walking back."

"That's sixteen miles. You must have started pretty early."

"Before the sun."

"Man! Everything I read warned against doing a round trip."

"That's why I *did* it," he laughed. "Cause they said I couldn't. But now," and here he looked out across the openness again for a long silent moment before finishing, "I can see why they said not to."

He stood up and brushed himself off. "Thanks for the snack and the water."

"Thanks for the chat. And good luck the rest of the way."

"Almost there!" Max said suddenly.

He looked at Max for a moment before answering. "That's right, Buffalo. Almost there." Then he turned back up the trail and said, "Seems like I've been 'almost there' for years."

LATER that night, after we cleaned up dinner at the campsite, we drove back to the park to find some place to shower and do a load of laundry. The boys and I stood in our shorts in line, clutching our towels, travel shampoo bottles, and a handful of quarters each to feed into the machine for seven minutes worth of water flow. A father and son went into the stalls before us and were babbling back and forth to one another in a language I couldn't recognize.

We waited our turn and after the boys and I finished, went to the car to look at the stars and wait for Theresa and Harper to come out. We sat on the bumper together comparing notes from the day. "It was weird to hear those people in there talking in another language," Henry said.

"Yeah," Max added, "even though I couldn't understand them, I could tell what they were saying just by the way they said it."

"Totally," Henry said.

"Oh yeah, what were they saying?" I asked.

Max slid off the bumper and turned to face us before dropping his voice into a muddled French accent (even though I'm pretty sure the father and son were not speaking French). "'Hurry up, dad! Pass me the shampoo before the water runs out! It's run out now, dad! Do you have any more money? I need another minute to wash the soap out.' That's when the father's hand came out from behind his curtain and passed quarters to the kid."

"Yeah. That's so weird." Henry said. "That's totally what they were saying."

"All I know is that it would suck to have to do all of this in another country," Max said.

"All of this?"

"Yeah, Dad, all of this," he waved his hand around. "Trying to figure out camping in a different *language*."

"That would be im*possible*," Henry said.

"Not impossible. We just saw people doing it."

"Okay, then, but, like, really hard."

"They're doing it though, aren't they? Just like us."

LATER that night, after I finished reading another chapter of Harry Potter aloud, helped Harper find her flashlight for the third time, and broke up the nightly tent tussle for space between Henry and Max, I lay silently on my back, looking up through the mesh tent top at the cloudy sky. Sometime before the silence gave way to sleep, my mind found its way to Simon Stimson, the dead drunken choir director from Thornton Wilder's, *Our Town*, a play I've taught only a handful of times in my teaching career.

There's a moment I like toward the end of the play, when Emily returns to her grave after witnessing, despite Stimson's warning not to, a day in her life through the eyes of the dead. Stimson rebukes her,

> *Yes, now you know. Now you know! That's what it was to be alive. To move about in a cloud of ignorance; to go up and down trampling on the feelings of those . . . of those about you. To spend and waste time as though you had a million years. To*

be always at the mercy of one self-centered passion, or another.
Now you know — that's the happy existence you wanted to go
back to. Ignorance and blindness.

But before Emily can answer the choirmaster, her mother-in-law, Mrs. Gibbs breaks in, "Simon Stimson, that ain't the whole truth and you know it." And that's what I kept thinking about as I lay there: the whole truth. Then Max nudged me with his elbow.

"I can't believe that guy ate your Cliff Bar," he said with his mouth just inches from my ear.

"He was hungry," I shrugged.

"I've never been *that* hungry."

"Me neither."

"When you offered it to him, did you really think he would take it?"

"I didn't think too much about it at the time. But I guess, no, I didn't think he would take it."

"Then why did you offer it to him?"

"Seemed like the right thing to do. He looked pretty hungry."

"Yeah, he looked like he was going to *die*."

"I can't believe he walked all that way in one day. I wonder why he did it," Max said.

"What, hike down and back in one day or eat my Cliff Bar?"

"Both."

"Well, like I said, Max, I think he was hungry."

"Yeah."

"There's lots of types of hunger," I said. Max nodded in reply, but he fell silent after that. I like to imagine he was thinking about the Whole Truth and all of that. But I can't say for sure what was on his mind. Either way, we didn't talk again until the morning.

Mother Road

(Day 8. The Grand Canyon — Henderson, NV)

THE NEXT MORNING I woke up both fast and slow — instantly aware of my surroundings and the day's work ahead of me, but at the same time unmoved by my typical morning urge to act. The world and I felt strangely aligned. No noise, and the only movement was a wind that blew fresh breaths into the corners of our still sleeping tent.

The sun shifted as I propped myself up on my elbow to better see my family. Just a little longer, I thought. Let me lay here undisturbed with the people I love most in the world. Preserve this moment. Let me never forget.

I'm not sure I know how to pray anymore. Can you still talk to God after you've been broken by her world? When I was little, I used to fold my hands and shut my eyes tight. The God I saw there was as clear to me as the face looking back from the mirror. It was an image sure and solid and wholly my own. I can still see it, but the steadiness it once gave me is gone now. Replaced by a presence I sometimes still feel, but can never quite manage to conjure when I need it most. Whatever that presence is, it was there with us that morning. There with me.

We were in a spaceship. The morning breeze luffed loose flaps as we hurtled through the galaxy at the slippery speed of time and space. Outside was another world. And I don't mean the dusty pine forest floor of the Ten X campground in the Kaibab National Forest, I mean the other universe where things like auto insurance payments and numbers on report cards feel like they matter. Where date nights devolve into parent-planning sessions, and the endless buzz of bad news out of Washington buries your face in your phone. Just a week after launching into the orbit of our trip, The World outside of our tent felt foolish, impractical, recklessly unsustainable and impossibly far away. "I never want to go back," I said to The Presence of the morning. And with those words my family began to stir.

An hour later, our campsite scoured clean, the Sequoia packed and primed with a tank full of gas, and our bellies bulging with a bagel and banana breakfast, we were standing together once again at the edge of the Grand Canyon.

IN the spring of 2015, my mother-in-law, Barbara, spent the weekend of Mother's Day at our house. We took a long walk together with the kids, stayed up late "chit-chatting" about nothing in particular, and enjoyed an unseasonably warm picnic dinner on our front porch. Later that night, we said our good-byes unceremoniously; she planned to come back in two weekends to watch the kids while Theresa and I ran the Buffalo half-marathon. But the day before she was scheduled to return to our place, she fell suddenly in her kitchen as she unpacked her groceries. And just like that, she was gone.

In this too-short, long lifetime, there is no telling how long we have to live and breathe and feel the scope of our humanity. How many chances we'll have to say I love you. How many times we'll be able to look each other in the eye and say good-bye. Theresa and I are both in our forties now. I can't say for sure if we'll ever get back to the Grand Canyon. I can't say anything for sure, really. So while we told the kids we came back that morning to snap a few more goofy posed pictures and stretch our legs a bit before settling in for a ride on Route 66, we were really there to say good-bye.

EVEN though there are faster ways to get from the Grand Canyon to Henderson, Nevada, we decided to slow roll it along Route 66 through the spotted countryside of rusty rhyming Burma Shave signs and other roadside kitsch. Along the way, Theresa and I annoyed the kids by playing Nat King Cole's *Route 66* about 17 times ("How was this song *ever* popular?!"), tried to connect the dots for the kids between the movie *Cars* and what we were seeing outside our windows, and did our best to resist the constant call to stop and shop at any of the countless namelessly nostalgic spots along the way between Seligman and Kingman, Arizona.

Once we crossed over into the Hualapai Indian Reservation, we stopped in the dusty heat for a roadside lunch of sandwiches under the shade of a makeshift shelter set up on the outskirts of an otherwise totally deserted town. The empty storefronts and broken windows of the old train station gave a ghostly vibe to the midafternoon heat, which shimmered up from the road in visible waves. To a rider, we were happy to leave the place behind, but I made a point to remind the kids that not everyone is as lucky as we are to see such places from the safe distance of our rearview mirror. Surely *some*body calls that place home. The kids just nodded silently to my sermon. It's impossible to know what sinks in. And so we drove on, "experiencing" Route 66 as all modern day nomads with a dinner date in Nevada do: from the inside of our air conditioned car.

The one exception we made to our No Stopping at Kitschy Places policy was the Hackberry General Store. I read *a lot* about this store while researching this stretch of the trip. One review used the terms "living museum," "Mother Road," "ghost town" and "America's Main Street" all in *the same sentence*. Such earnestness is pretty compelling. Still I probably wouldn't have felt the need to stop if my old teaching buddy, John Shafer, hadn't once told me of his desire to, upon his death, have his ashes flushed down a toilet in Grand Central Station. "What better way to get yourself out there?" he asked with a shrug one day in the hall before class. Upon his untimely death, his wife, Susan, thankfully, did not take this request seriously. Still buddies and wives play different roles in people's lives, so, in a nod to John's theory of deathly distribution, and with a wink toward family trip karma, we pulled into the parking lot of the Hackberry General Store so I could give them a couple of copies of my novel to sell on their shelves. What better way to get yourself out there?

We had fun poking around the aisles, looking at the license plates, and playing with all the trinkets. The manager looked at me like I was crazy when I told her I wanted to give her two of my books free of charge to sell in her store. "You don't want any *money* for them?" she asked.

"No, just knowing they're for sale here is enough for me," I said without a trace of irony.

"Nah," she shook her head, "everybody wants some*thing*."

"Not me," I said. "I'm all set."

"Okay. Suit yourself." She turned back to the register and muttered to the cashier, "Sure does take all kinds," before handing over my books. "Write these up and get 'em on the shelf."

BUZZING along The Mother Road, we were making better time than expected and soon realized that, at our current rate, we were due to arrive in Henderson much earlier than anticipated. With time to pass, we decided to take a quick look at Lake Mead before paying a visit to the Hoover Dam. We figured with these added stops and a visit to the store for groceries on the way, we'd arrive at our destination in Henderson just in time for dinner.

LAKE Mead was created in the 1930s when the Colorado River was slowed and rerouted during the building of the Hoover Dam. In this way water (and electricity), usually in short supply in the area, was redistributed to otherwise arid and dead places. Soon a budding scene was born.

The heat of the day was stifling, well over 100 degrees, when we pulled into Lake Mead's roadside outlook. The scene felt like a photograph taken on another planet. A red rock, burnt-out bowl with stagnant water reflecting back a thick foam of heavy gray clouds that hung like a headache in the sky.

The banks of Lake Mead are marked with stratified stains. When I asked a man who, like us, was standing by the front of his car looking out over the lake, what the stains were from he said, "Those aren't stains. Those are watermarks. That's how high the lake used to be before everything started drying up around here. Been a bunch of years of drought. I've lived here my whole life. This," he waved his hand across the scene in front of us, "is something out of a movie. You can't believe how low the water's gotten."

"Wow, in just a few years then?" I asked.

"Yeah, just a few years ago, the lake was as high as that top mark. 'Bathtub Rings' they call them." He pointed with a finger to the top ridge of darkened lines that rimmed the water on all sides. "Whole thing is just drying up. You kids are lucky to see it." He smiled at Harper, but she looked away. Then he turned to me. "I've got a daughter too. She used to be shy just like that, but now . . . watch out! Tell you what, my daughter used to swim here all the time. Trust me, your kids will be grateful they got to see this before it's all gone."

We followed the assuring voice of the Sequoia's navigational system through the twisting branches of highway that lead from Lake Mead to the Hoover Dam. While the lake is a depressing reminder of the toll of climate change, the dam is the type of man-made manipulative magic that is both stunning to behold and heartbreakingly sad.

The Hoover Dam harnesses the once mighty Colorado River, the beauty of which we saw from afar just the day before, for human needs. The Colorado, whose currents carved the Grand Canyon, now flows flaccidly, a neutered and stilled shell of itself, lapping listlessly against the smooth, well-formed concrete of man's best effort to tame it. Looking at the Hoover Dam, you get the feeling that we humans, this planet's most pervasive invasive species, will continue to torture and destroy every sacred space we have until there is nothing left for us to ruin.

And as if all of this existential threat shit weren't enough, as we slowly made our way out onto the walking path that rims the edge of the dam's concrete horseshoe, I couldn't help but obsessively notice that the only thing separating my very curious kids from giving into gravity and plunging to their deaths down the steep slopes of this man-made hell hole was a waist-high wall and iron railing. I know, I know, just yesterday we walked nearly a mile down a steep cliff edge with no railing or wall to speak of and I wasn't really that worried. But I can't explain it. The Canyon just felt safer.

And did I mention that it was oppressively hot? Like no breeze, locked inside an oven hot, hot?

Sure, it was neat to stand by the marker in the middle of the dam indicating the state line between Arizona and Nevada; we got a couple of cool shots of that, but as for the rest of the experience, as far as I'm concerned, you engineering types can keep the whole damn thing. Good luck with that.

Max — astride the Nevada Arizona state line atop the Hoover Dam. Boulder City, Nevada.

LIKE most things, when you first start Adulting, you think you're better at it than you actually are. You master a few meals, figure out how to not shrink your shirts, pay all of your bills on time for a couple of months in a row, and then you start thinking, "I got this. What's all the fuss?" This is usually when something happens like you getting food poisoning because you made your burger with the grayish-green meat you found in the back of the fridge and you didn't check its internal temperature before you ate it. Or you put all of your towels and your sweaters in the washing machine at the same time because they're all blue — and later you come down stairs to find that the door to the machine has popped open, the basement is partially flooded, and your clothes and towels are still soaking wet because the spin cycle was aborted by the machine's emergency shut off valve. Or you realize that for three months now you've been paying your landlord's cable bill, which is much more expensive than yours because all she does is sit on her ass and watch TV while you actually work for a living, and she's been paying your basic rate all because the mail carrier keeps delivering her mail to you because she used to live in the downstairs apartment, and you didn't bother to pay attention to the name on the bill, because . . . well because double checking that sort of thing is something your *father* told you to always do right before you started Adulting, and you were too busy telling him "I've got it under control, Dad!" to bother to listen. You see what I mean? Point is, Adulting is harder than it looks.

Once we determined the final route of our trip, I reached out on Facebook to see if there was anyone with a washing machine and functioning shower who lived along our route between parks who would be willing to put up with a stinky family of five and their camp-caked clothes for a night. I figured this would be an easy way to cut down on lodging cost and give me the added bonus of touching base with a long lost friend or two. A former student of mine, Noah Kohl, was one of only a few people who responded. "Hey Mr. Bindig, I live in Las Vegas if that helps during your travels. We have a spare room, too, with its own bathroom."

I shot back: "Hey Noah, We'd love to take you up on it. If possible, we'd love to crash for one night and depart early the next morning. It'd be my wife (Theresa) and our three kids: Henry (13), Max (10), and Harper (7). All we're looking for is a roof over our heads, a place to shower, and maybe a chance to do some laundry. Sleeping on the floor is no big deal. Let me know if you think this could work. Thanks, <u>Matt</u> Bindig." One of the hardest things for the former students I'm in touch with is to get used to the idea of calling me, Matt. It's crazy. I've run into thirty year olds with kids and careers who still insist on calling me "Mr. Bindig." I guess it makes sense that there would be a little social awkwardness in such a relationship, and I was prepared to deal with that when crashing at Noah's. But mostly I was proud of him for being brave enough to offer to put us up, and super grateful for a chance to shower and wash our clothes after a few nights "out at camp".

I called Noah when we arrived at the apartment complex and both he and Abby greeted us at the Sequoia with happy, familiar hugs that made us feel instantly at home. They helped us schlep our stuff up the stairs, and both of them chatted up the kids while Theresa and I settled the room and started our wash. When I came back into the living room, Henry and Noah were talking about soccer and I was struck by the fact that they are closer in age than Noah and I.

Frozen Veggie Lasagna (ah, a staple of my early Adulting career — well not the veggie version, just the lasagna) was served for dinner, and they didn't even care that the kids sat on their carpet with their plates on their laps while they ate.

While our kids cycled through their showers, we told Noah and Abby about our trip so far and they talked about the start of their respective careers. After college, Noah moved out to the Vegas area hoping his family connections might help him catch on as a cop. They didn't, so now he's working on becoming an EMT. Abby works crazy hours as an orthopedic physician's assistant.

When Theresa and I ducked in to take our showers and fold our clothes, Noah and Abby found a fun show for the kids to watch on TV. Right before bed, Noah and I had a beer together (he cracked them open using the old butt-of-your-hand-against-the-cap while wedging it against the edge of a countertop technique) while he told my kids funny stories about having me as his teacher. My kids seemed astonished to hear that I could be something to someone other than a dad.

Before we crashed we made our morning plans (Abby had to go to work early, so Noah would take us out to his favorite pancake house). Then we tucked the kids in as the last load of laundry came out of the dryer.

As I lay in bed that night, drunk with exhaustion, my family snoring beside me, my dehydrated brain on the brink of buzzing from two beers, I kept thinking about Noah and Abby and the life they were just starting. Living it out here in the desert.

The next day was set to be our longest day of driving. Eight or more hours depending. Vegas. Death Valley. Then back to California and Sequoia National Park. But then each day is a long road regardless of where you are heading. Tomorrow wasn't about The Strip, The Desert or Making it Back to the Mountains Before Dark. It was about the hum of the tires and the faces we'd meet along the way. As I slipped into sleep, I kept thinking it's amazing what you learn once you figure out who you ought to be listening to.

Hard Good

(Day 9. Henderson, NV — Sequoia)

TURNS OUT NOAH'S FAVORITE breakfast place, Baby Stacks, serves food worth lingering over. So with plates full of s'mores pancakes in front of us, we delayed our departure an extra hour before finally bidding Noah good-bye. With our arms full of parcels of leftover pancakes, we climbed into the car and headed for the Vegas strip.

Even though my kids were sufficiently impressed by the Sphinx, stunned by the show girl they saw opening a door in her sequined costume and cap, and briefly believed that the architectural model in front of the Paris casino was indeed the real Eiffel Tower, the thing they'll probably remember most from our drive through Vegas was the "salute" Theresa and I gave to the Trump International Hotel. It's not often we gesture and speak in such ways in front of our kids (well, that's true for Theresa anyway), but something in the moment seemed to call for our own special version of "Hail to the Chief."

Henry, who up to that point was madly snapping pictures to send to his friends, lowered his phone long enough to ask, "Why is *his* name up there?"

"It's all gold," Harper said, twirling her hand over her head. "Is that even real?" Turns out the mostly glass surface of the Trump hotel *is* infused with real gold, which is why it glitters so gaudily in the desert sun.

"I don't know, buddy. But either way, can you tell that it's obviously very important to our president to *seem* like the richest guy in town? Kinda sad huh?"

"Yeah. But *is* he the richest guy?" Harper asked.

"Depends on who you ask, sweetheart," Theresa said.

"And what you mean by *rich*." I replied

"All I know is that he sure does like big buildings," Max added.

"And money," Harper said with a nod.

"Bling, bling, bling," Henry snapped his fingers against the window, and clicked his tongue in tune as we turned back onto the highway. It only took a few minutes for the shine of the strip to recede in the rearview.

A wild burro. Bullfrong Mining District. Beatty, Nevada.

WE stuck to Route 95 as we drove north out of Las Vegas. Making time through Indian Springs and Amargosa Valley, before finally stopping for lunch two hours later in Beatty.

Beatty, Nevada, once a thriving, Old West mining town has gained a measure of fame over the years because of their wild donkey population. Legend has it, when the miners skipped town, they left many of their burros behind to fend for themselves. Absent any natural predators, the wild burro population has grown at a steady rate ever since, leaving locals alternately bemused and frustrated by the swelling numbers of these mostly docile, but sometimes-salty, beasts.

Once in Beatty, we pulled to the side of some nameless dirt road, just off the main drag, to eat our lunches in our laps. And there, clustered in the shade of a tree less than a hundred yards away were a bunch of the old boys. It was an odd sight to say the least. Back home it's very common to see deer spotting the countryside at twilight. So it's not as if I haven't had to contend with wild creatures lingering about in a mostly human habitat. No, it wasn't their presence that was weird to me, as much as the fact that they were *donkeys*. I guess it's just what you get used to.

Harper rolled down her window and let the August heat pour into the car. Being midday it was well into the 90s. The sound of her munching must have caught their attention because the bravest of the burros slowly lumbered over to the Sequoia to get a better look. He stopped just a few feet from Harper's open window, his strangely human eyes beseeching her as his nose probed the air. "Can I feed him, Dad? Can I give him the rest of my apple?"

When I was kid, a friend of mine visited African Lion Safari, an animal reservation slash theme park just over the Canadian border in Cambridge, Ontario. He bragged at lunch for weeks about the upcoming trip, but when he returned to our table after spring break, it was to tell the story of some breed of monkey trying to rip the windshield wiper off his father's car. Worse, another one almost cost his brother, who was foolish enough to offer the critter a potato chip, his left eye. "Better not feed him, Harper. I'd hate to give him the wrong idea."

"I won't give him an idea, just the rest of my apple," she said, her forehead wrinkled in confusion. I rolled up her window in reply. "Dad, come on! He's so cute."

"It's the cute ones you've got to be careful of."

"Oh, God," Henry moaned. "Here we go again with the 'Girl Power' talk."

THE day after Harper was born, while the boys ate breakfast with my father, I went to the local grocery store to pick up a plant and balloon to take to Theresa at the hospital. As I waited for the cashier to ring out my stuff, my eyes fell upon a copy of *Cosmopolitan* magazine prominently propped in the rack in front of me at eye level. Dakota Fanning's face smiled back at me from the glossy cover, sandwiched between the headlines: *His Best Sex Ever* and *"Um, vagina, are you okay down there?"* Lower on the page it said: *25 Girlie things to start doing again* and across the bottom: *Too Naughty to Say Here!* *But You Have to Try This Sex Trick*. What the fuck was this? Did the folks at Cosmo forget that just the night before my baby girl came into the world? Who the hell were *they* to fill her head with this trash?

"Are these magazines usually kept here?" I asked the twelve-year-old girl chopping her gum as she scanned my items (when did they start letting twelve-year-olds work the cash register?).

"Oh, Cosmo? Yeah, we always keep them there. Why?"

I caught myself just before slipping into a sermon about sexualization, objectification and the dangers of defining pleasure on other peoples' terms. The last thing I needed the day after my daughter was born, was to get arrested for screaming at a store clerk about the impact of magazine smut on the psyche of young girls. "It's just, I've got a daughter now," I said.

"Don't worry," the girl said. "She'll probably start with *Seventeen* before she gets to *Cosmo*. You've got time."

"That's reassuring."

But the truth is, time is *not* on Harper's side.

At seven, she is brave and fierce, willing to stand up for herself whether with her words or her fists. She loves to draw, climb, decorate her room and do cartwheels. Her favorite song is "Divorce-Separation Blues" by the Avett Brothers because of the cool yodeling Seth does after the chorus. When I read her Harry Potter, she doesn't seem to feel any obligation to name Hermione as her favorite character just because she's a girl. She loves to snuggle *and* ride her bike.

But the world is coming for her.

Soon her friends will start taking selfies in skimpy bathing suits. *You're so gorgeous!* Harper will peck into her phone in reply.

Soon some dude will ask her to "send pictures" and if she doesn't she'll be labeled a prude, a tease, or worse. And if she does, all the girls will call her a whore, and all the boys will pass the phone around the locker room and point out her "flaws."

Soon she'll start listening to "performers" instead of songwriters, and tearing her clothes on purpose, and keeping her hand down in class because she doesn't want Dominic or David or Dan to feel threatened because she's smarter than them. She'll act like she cares when they talk about video games, and she'll lower her voice when she talks with her friends about her favorite books. In gym class, she'll try not to break a sweat.

That is what this world does to girls.

Even cool girls with Moms who don't put on make-up everyday

and don't have to wear skinny jeans to feel attractive and young. Moms, who would never think of getting Botox to "Plump their lips for the party."

Even tough girls, whose brothers don't own any kid gloves. Who never once treat their little sister like anything other than "one of the guys."

Even smart girls with Dads who aren't afraid to call bullshit when other moms say things like, "He's just pushed you because he *likes* you." Dads who proudly call themselves Feminist.

Even with all of that, this world will still crush her. And there's nothing I can do about it.

I rolled down her window. "You can give him the apple if you want to, Harper. It's okay. I'm sorry." But the burro was already walking away.

THE Bare Mountain range ran along the horizon next to us as we were headed into Death Valley, the hottest place on planet Earth. We drove into the park on roads cut into the surrounding mountains at rollercoaster angles. Red rock, sand, and clusters of creosote bushes undulated for miles before us in the blazing heat of the valley floor. We arrived at 1:00 p.m..

In August, at that time of day, the average temperature in the valley is 114 degrees. Once inside the park, we pulled over and climbed out of the Sequoia just to breathe the air.

"It's almost like we're under siege out here," I said to no one in particular.

"What's that mean?" Harper asked.

"Like people are coming to get us."

"But we're the only ones here."

"Not people then," I said. "*Forces.*"

"Forces? What do you mean?"

I walked out to the double yellow lines that ran through the middle of the empty road. No cars were coming; we would be able to see them long before they arrived if there were. I fell to my knees, tipped my head back to the clouds and raised my arms in a dramatic posture of distress before opening my mouth to let out a scream of desperate despair. Harper giggled with delight.

"See what I mean?" I asked her as I climbed to my feet. "There are forces. Everything in the universe is trying to crush us."

"You're weird, Dad."

"Maybe, but that doesn't mean I'm not right," I said as I poked her in the belly. Theresa and the boys were already walking back to the car. "What else do you think happened to the cars that left those tire tracks?" I pointed to the black lines that snaked in semi-circles on the tar behind us. "The forces got 'em."

"Why did you just kneel and scream in the road?"

"Because it's hard to fight the forces. It takes a toll on you. But I wanted to let them know that I'm not gonna quit. No way." Harper looked back toward where I was kneeling a minute ago. I could tell she was thinking.

"Go ahead," I said. "You try." She giggled again. "There are no cars coming. Go ahead and let 'em know you've got no plans to give up anytime soon. Let 'em know Harper is here to stay!"

To my great surprise she marched out to the middle of the road and turned toward me. There was an odd smile on her face. She let out a little laugh and raised her arms to the sun. Then as the wind tossed her hair, my daughter tipped her head back and let out a scream of hope.

I'M not sure what compels a person to do something "just to say that they did it." Maybe it's bragging rights. Maybe it's a way to keep testing yourself, to make sure that you haven't gone stale. "Yep, I did that once. I've been there. Looks like this here lame duck's still got some quack in him." If I'm being honest, I know, for me, my desire to go to Death Valley was at least partially about that. But it was also about the survival metaphor.

Pacing the ground. Breathing the air. Seeing the ragged landscape with my own two eyes. Experiencing one of the most hostile climates on the face of this earth, even if just for a moment, and being able to say I *survived*. Wouldn't living such an experience give a person a passport of perspective through future suffering? Couldn't I now say, somewhere down the road, "Alright then, I'll give you this is pretty bad, but I've seen worse. I've been to the Valley. I've stood at the crossroads of Hell on earth, and drove out a few hours later, intact." This world cannot break me.

I want to be able to pass that sense of assurance on to my kids.

Now I'm not sure if padding across the sand dunes of Mesquite Flats in flip-flops for five minutes gave us the right to say all *that*, but metaphorically, that's what I was looking for.

To take a straight-line path from where we were in Death Valley to the Lodgepole Campground in the northern outreach of Sequoia National Forest where we were scheduled to sleep that night would have taken just a few short hours. Unfortunately no such straight-line route exists.

So I put the music on low, refilled my water bottle, and silently drove a ragged U of road past the likes of Stovepipe Wells, Searles Valley, and Bakersfield, California stopping only for gas before heading North again toward the mountains and towering trees of Sequoia National Park.

We stopped for a late dinner at a Burger King (our first fast food of the trip). After ordering our food, I left Theresa and the kids sitting on the sidewalk outside to gobble down their grease while I scooted over to fill up the tank hoping, in both cases, that this would be enough fuel to get us through the next leg of the trip. Twenty minutes later, we passed the entrance to Sequoia National Park, snapping a picture of the kids next to the sign to commemorate the moment. It was 7:51 p.m.. We didn't get to our campsite until after 9:30.

WE spent the last hour and a half of the trip driving up a steep, unfamiliar mountain road whose hairpin switchbacks left my forearms burning. Curtains of darkness descended upon us as our headlights disappeared around the twisting bends. More than that, a growing sense of unspoken dread filled the silence between Theresa and me. It was very dark. Everyone was fried. It was going to take a certain amount of critical energy to set up camp. We didn't really know where we were going. And we were in bear country. Did I mention it was very dark?

We passed by a well-lit ranger station and drove into the blackness of the campground proper, a tunnel of headlights leading the way. By some combination of luck, planning and navigational skill, we eventually found our reserved site.

Everything I'd read about the park warned that the bear population was not to be taken lightly. So as I set up the tent, Theresa and the kids changed out of their food-close clothes and put them, along with all of our food, bathing supplies, and anything else that might have a discernible scent to it, into the locked bear box tucked into the corner of our site.

We were just about to climb into our tent for the night when an urgent voice called, "Folks! Folks!" A jaunty young man in a crisp ranger uniform walked briskly toward us, touching the wide brim of his hat with one hand and shining his flashlight at our feet with the other. "Just wanted to let you know that if you hear any gunshots, don't be alarmed."

"What? Jesus!" Theresa grabbed my hand and Harper shuffled behind my legs.

"We've got a *problem* bear in the vicinity," the ranger nodded somewhat breathlessly. There was no doubt he was enjoying the concern in Theresa's eyes. "Now don't worry, Miss, I'm not going to shoot to kill. Just rubber bullets. But if you should find that he's gotten close to you just shout, *GET OUT! BEAR! BEAR! BEAR!* as loud as you can. That usually scares him off. Either way I'll be around and probably will hear you, so just sit tight."

He looked at me, "Make sense, sir?"

"Yes, we got it. Thank you."

"That's all then." He moved on to tell our neighbors.

"DAD, there's a *bear*," Max said. "You always wanted to see one."

"True, buddy, but maybe not tonight."

"But the guy said he was right around here," Henry implored. "We should just do a quick lap to look for him."

"What? No! Mom, make them stop."

"Boys, you're upsetting your sister. Now let's just get into the tent and settle in."

"Matt, do you think we've got everything cleaned up and locked in like we're supposed to? Are we all set?"

"Yeah, we're good," I assured her. "All we've got to do is fall asleep. This'll be easy."

INSIDE the spaceship, we crawled into our sleeping bags. Even though it was August, at this elevation it would dip down as low as 40 degrees by morning. I could see my breath as I kissed Theresa and the kids goodnight.

It took about seventeen seconds for me to fall asleep. Even with the ranger's words ringing in my ears; I was too exhausted to worry. Usually when I fall asleep like that it means I'm out until morning unless a bomb goes off next to my head or something. And if I do wake up, it takes me like an *hour* before I'm fully cognizant. When the kids were really little and used to wake up in the middle of the night to nurse, I sometimes would go in ahead of Theresa and change their diapers, and in the morning, I'd have absolutely no recollection of ever doing it. Nothing bad ever happened. It's not like I dropped them or anything. It's just I wouldn't remember *any* of it. Even conversations Theresa and I had. My brain just doesn't have a quick "On" switch when I'm super tired. This time though, by some miracle, when Theresa called my name with fear in her voice, I woke up right away.

Maybe it was because I had just fallen asleep. Maybe it was because we were out in the middle of nowhere near the top of a mountain with a problem bear and a trigger-happy ranger wandering around, or maybe it was because I was being water-boarded by my son's vomit. "Max! What the hell!"

"Sorry!" Tears. Gag. Spit. Choke. Another splash shot out of him this time the bulk of it fell onto my sleeping bag and pillow instead of my face.

"Open the tent, Matt! Open the tent!" Theresa pushed Max and me out into the cold night air as another wave of puke hit the ground. I grabbed Max by the shoulders and directed him away from the tent.

Max, covered in regurgitated burger and fries, looked impossibly small as he stood sobbing in my arms. "My ears! My ears!"

All of my kids are pretty tough, but Max, more than all of them, almost never cries because of physical pain. I mean, it takes *a lot*. Like this one time, he must have been eight or so, he ran into Theresa while we were riding bikes together and flew over the handlebars, landing painfully on his side in the street. Theresa's inertia and Max's sudden movement was too much to take in, so without wanting to (obviously) Theresa promptly rode over both of Max's legs — buhlump, buhlump — as they splayed out there before her. Even then, it was *Theresa* who almost started crying. Max was fine. That's what I'm talking about. So to see him crying seemingly because he threw up in the tent, told me something else was seriously wrong.

"Max, come on. It's cold. Are you all done?" Let me get you to the car." I could hear Theresa scurrying about behind me, but I paid her no heed. All of my attention was on Max. Once I got him to the car, I found a bath towel and wiped him down the best I could. Then I used the other side to clean myself up. I peeled Max out of his clothes and was turning back to the tent, when something sharp grabbed my back,

It was Mama bear. Mama bear, Theresa, that is.

"Has he stopped?" Max sat in the driver's seat in his underwear, crying softly now. "Maxie, what's wrong?"

"My ears!" Suddenly, he was at full froth again.

"Get out of those clothes, Matt. You're covered in puke."

"Why are you freaking out?"

She turned to me with abject horror in her eyes, "There's a *fucking* bear out here, Matt! That's why I'm freaking out. What do you think it'll do when it smells all this . . . all this . . . food?"

It took about two seconds for me to get to the tent. Turns out there was nothing to worry about. In the time it took me to get Max undressed, Theresa deployed some serious mother magic. The tent was clear of vomit. The only sign of what happened was a pile of soiled sleeping bags, pillows, and a spent towel lumped outside of the open tent flap. Harper and Henry were safe inside, sound asleep.

My wife is amazing.

"Okay. I'll get a garbage bag out of the back of the car. We'll lock all this stuff in the bear box with the food and figure the rest out in the morning."

"But, Matt, look at yourself. You're covered in vomit. You've got to take everything off."

BAMPF! BAMPF! BAMPF! The car alarm. Our headlights flashing into our neighbors' tents. Max standing in front of the opened door. *BAMPF! BAMPF! BAMPF!*

"Max! The alarm! Shut the door!"

"My ears!" he cradled his head. "My ears!"

"What the hell is wrong with him?" Theresa ignored me, ran to Max, shut the car up and managed to calm him down enough to get him back into the driver's seat and out of the cold. I stripped down to my shorts and crammed my clothes plus the pile of soiled stuff into a garbage bag and shoved it all into the bear box.

When I got back to the car, I found that Theresa had dug out a t-shirt and shorts for both Max and me. "I know it's cold," she said, her teeth clicking against each other, "But this is all I could find."

"My ears!"

"Jesus, Matt, what's wrong with him?"

"I bet it's the altitude. Get in the tent. We'll sleep in the car. I've got this. Henry and Harper need you. Keep them safe from the bear." I think it was the bear reference that finally convinced her to go.

"We got this, Max," I said as I climbed in with him. "We're good. Dad's here." But after a half an hour of Max toggling between sleep and tears, it was pretty clear he wasn't okay.

I unzipped the tent and shook Theresa awake. "I'm going to see if I can get back to the ranger station. I think Max has altitude sickness. I don't know enough about it to know whether it's serious or not and I can't get any service on my phone. He's really hurting. I need to find some help. A ranger will know what to do."

"Matt, are you sure? Do you think you'll be able to find it?"

"I have to, Theresa. For Max."

"Are you okay to drive?"

"I'll be back."

OTHER than at the ranger's station and the central latrine, there were no lights on at the Lodgepole campground. Moreover, because the campsites are designed with maximum capacity in mind, the paths that pass for roads twist through the trees in dizzyingly disorienting circles, oftentimes with a tent tucked unsuspectedly behind an unprotected bend. But I drove slowly and followed the path as best as I could. It took a few tries, but eventually I found the ranger station, a one-story cabin, the front of which was no bigger than most people's garage. I pulled in next to what looked like the main entrance, shut off the Sequoia's headlights, and kept the engine running. Max was quiet now. His eyes half open. His body shivered and curled into the seat.

"Max, buddy, I'm going to go see if I can find anyone to help us. Do you think you're going to get sick again?" He shook his head. "All done? You sure?"

"Yes."

"Do you want to come with me, or do you want to stay in the car?

"Stay."

"Okay, but I'm going to lock the doors, so don't try to open them. I've got the keys. Stay put." He nodded again and curled into a tighter ball underneath the towel.

Walking away from that car into the soundless night was one of the scariest things I've ever done. It wasn't scary because it was cold and dark and I was in bear country wearing shorts, a t-shirt and flip-flops that I'm pretty sure still had some barf on them. It wasn't scary because the blue light glowing from a computer inside an office I found around the back of the ranger station reminded me of that scene from *Silence of the Lambs* where Buffalo Bill cuts open the cocoon and talks to the face of larva in a garbled voice. And it wasn't scary because Max was alone in a locked car, out of earshot. How easy it would be for some deranged stranger to break into that car and take him away without me being able to get to him? No, what was scary was that my son was hurting and in desperate need of help. He was counting on me. He believed that I would find a way to save him. But there wasn't any help coming. I was all alone. And I didn't have the slightest idea what to do.

BAMPF! BAMPF! BAMPF! The car alarm screamed into the night. *BAMPF! BAMPF! BAMPF!*

As I rounded the corner of the building at a full sprint I saw Max shivering in the slice of light from the open passenger door. "Where were you, Dad?! My ears! They hurt so much!"

"Get back in the car, buddy," I said. We've got to get you back into town." I buckled him in and turned The Sequoia toward the same mountain road we climbed a lifetime ago earlier that evening. "I've got to drive you back down the mountain, Max." And I truly believe I would have driven the 90 minutes back down to civilization, or tried to anyway, if Max, suddenly awake and calm, hadn't grabbed my arm.

"Dad, you can't. You're too tired. Let's just go back. I can make it. The pain is getting better. Let's just go to sleep."

"Max, I've got to get you some help."

"Take me back," he said. "I want to go back to camp."

"Are you sure, buddy?"

"Yes. Don't leave. You're tired."

"I'm fine, Max." He curled into a ball again, closed his eyes, and shook his head.

"Go back, Dad."

I'm not sure how long we sat there, headlights pointing out into the night, engine humming, the only sound our ragged breaths, before I finally decided. "We'll go back now, okay? We'll go back to Mom." Once I turned the car around, it took me almost 40 minutes to find our campsite again. I shut off the lights as I pulled in.

Max was sleeping restlessly, so I left him where he was and crept over to the tent to let Theresa know we were back. When I opened the flap, I saw that they were all huddled together in a mass against the opposite side of the tent. Safe.

When I got back to the car, I opened the trunk and lowered the seats as much as I could around our gear. Then I shook Max awake and brought him to the back to lay down.

"I'm cold." All we had in the car with us was the one towel he was wrapped in.

"Here," I said, curling my body around him like a C. "Tuck into me. Here's the towel. I'll keep you warm." Soon the overhead light shut off. A little while later, Max started to snore.

I didn't sleep more than an hour. I just lay there with my boy in my arms. Trying to keep him warm with my own heat.

Just after five o'clock in the morning, Max started to stir. I went to the tent and woke Theresa. "I need to trade places until the kids wake up."

"What happened?" she asked. "You're back."

"Yes. I didn't want to wake you."

"What time did you get back? Did you find any help? Is Max okay?" Her hands were on my chest. "I'm sorry I fell asleep."

"It was late. I don't know what time it was exactly. But we didn't find any help. We just helped each other."

"Oh my God, Matt. That was so hard."

"Yeah. It was. But it's all good now, Theresa. We're all good."

And we *were* good too. I wasn't just saying it.

This world cannot break us.

What About Me?
(Day 10. Sequoia — Kings Canyon)

THE WEIRDEST PART OF being a parent for me is even though it's objectively clear that "It's not about you anymore," *you* are still there. Kind of like an aging once-superstar who is slowly being phased out of the starting rotation. But if you want to stay sane, you can't take this fact out and look at it too much. Cause if you do, if you allow yourself a few, "But what about mes?" Things can get away from you *real fast*. You let yourself go down that road, even just a little bit, and before you know it your kids are writing their college essay about how their high school football coach filled the void left by their dad who was never around anyway, and when he was, he was usually four-beers-drunk, watching sports on the couch, just because he needed a break from it all.

Still the "What about mes?" can happen sometimes.

Like, just for example, when you're woken up early by the birds in Sequoia National Park after spending a nearly sleepless night wrapped around a squirming ten year old in the half-folded down back seat of a rented Toyota Sequoia, shivering under a threadbare towel and haunted by the fear that a "problem bear" following the smell of your aforementioned son's vomit-drenched sleeping bag will maul your wife and other two children as they sleep soundly in their tent. What about me?

I could have easily woken up and said, Fuck it. I need a break. Forget the kids wanting breakfast. Forget finding laundry facilities. Forget packing up the car and camp. Forget the whole damn day and the batch of memories we're sure to make. Shoot, forget even my sweet, beautiful wife and the hug she needs this morning. The whispered reassurance that Max is okay. What about me? What about what *I* need?

I need some sleep! Or a nice hearty breakfast at least. A few minutes alone with my wife in the tent wouldn't be so bad either. And after that, an hour or so to catalogue my thoughts, uninterrupted in my journal, just like Henry Fuckin' Thoreau. How about that? What about me?

But I'm a *dad* and a *husband*, so instead I crawled out of the tent and guzzled down two cups of crappy instant coffee. Then I mixed up a bowl of lukewarm oatmeal (how many days in a row has it been now?), and sent the kids, including Max who, much to my amazement seemed *totally fine*, off to hunt native lizards on a nearby rocky outcropping, while I battled a squad of savvy squirrels who twice tipped over our cooler as I tried to roll up the tent and repack the car. Meanwhile, Theresa fed quarters into the washing machine by the ranger station, hoping we had enough cash to ensure clean bedding to sleep in the next night.

SCIENTISTS now believe that, though separate, trees can communicate with each other through a network of fungi, sort of like an underground brain, warning each other of dangers and helping each other to not only survive, but thrive. In this way trees both work toward their own survival and to collectively ensure the future of the forest as a whole. Married couples are a lot like trees.

IT was late morning by the time we finished reviewing the park map and set our course for the day's hikes. With an eye on Max's hydration and energy level we rolled out of the Lodgepole campground not necessarily ready, but at least hopeful about whatever the day would bring.

GIANT Sequoia trees are the largest trees in the world by volume. They grow singularly or in small clusters and their reddish-orange bark makes them stand out from their peers as if cast in a spotlight shown down by God. Three times on our way to the trailhead, I pulled over to the side of the road so we could get out and mingle with one of these miracles shining bright in the morning sun. The children stood with their backs against one, their arms fully spread, fingers touching like the paper dolls you make in kindergarten when you first learn how to use scissors. Wide as my kids collectively stood, there was still a good eight feet of the tree's circumference that went untouched by their hands.

Later as we walked along the trail to The Roosevelt Tree, sun slanting through the towering branches, the morning air both crisp and somehow ripe with the coming heat of the day, the children gathered football-sized pine cones like eggs on Easter morning. Laughing together in wonder at the joy they found in their discoveries. They took turns ducking into closet-sized grooves in claw-footed root structures and jumping out to scare one another as they raced around the feet of giants.

Everything is made to flicker these days. To catch our attention at a glance and hold it with endorphin blasts of pinged affirmation. How many followers do you have? Who added you on your birthday? Where are you on the Snap Map?

But these trees, on this planet long before Christ wove his way into the human story, care nothing of the foolish things that dictate our days. These trees have seen great men come and go. They stood stoically by as machines marched across the face of the planet consuming everything in their path. They sniffed the scorched wind as The Bomb's blast turned whole cities to dust in the name of a flag. And they remain. Against all odds, they are here. There is more wonder in one of their branches than in all the universities of the world.

Henry and Harper — beholding the wonder of a fallen sugar pinecone. Sequoia National Park.

MORO ROCK is a great granite outcropping that stands 6,725 feet above sea level. From its highest point you can turn to see both the whole of the San Joaquin Valley and the snow-dusted Sierra Nevada mountain range, known as the Great Western Divide, which forms the border between Sequoia National Park and Kings Canyon. From the vantage point of the Rock's topmost outlook, the Generals Highway looks more like an ant trail than a major road carved into the side of the canyon. But we knew exactly none of this as we began to climb the 350 steps that snake along the Rock's narrow trail constructed by the National Park service in 1931. Instead our minds were full of the two sister emotions that make life worth living: wonder and fear.

There are times when the Moro Rock trail narrows to a width that can only accommodate one human form. Occasionally, on the way to the top, we encountered hikers making their way down. When this happened, we stepped back and pressed our backs against the craggy, damp surface as strangers passed less than a hand's width away from our faces.

Such moments are wonderful opportunities to consider the stomach dropping, vertical plunge that whispers to you from the other side of the Thank God handrail (I named it that) that separates the trail from certain death.

True to form, Max, still a bit peaky from the night before, took the climb in stride. There were a few times he stopped to re-adjust his grip on the Thank God handrail, but if he was scared, he didn't show it. He had a climber's reputation to uphold.

Harper was seemingly too busy talking to Theresa to notice the razor's edge on which we walked. I'll give Theresa at least partial credit for this. As Harper blathered on about trees and mountains and the big black bird that just flew by, Theresa wore the tense smile of motherhood. You know the smile I'm talking about? Lips pursed just slightly, cheeks set in a Cheshire Cat grin to hide clenched teeth. The whole idea is if you keep your eyes bright and your mouth set just so, your kids will have no idea that you too are scared shitless. This is an essential posture to learn if you ever hope to convince your children to do anything remotely challenging. People like to say that dogs and bees can smell fear; in my experience, the same is true of kids. You can't let 'em sniff ya.

Anyway, if fear indeed has a smell, then all the bears in the San Joaquin valley were likely to have turned their noses to Moro Rock that August morning because Henry was not enjoying himself one bit. I mean, he was *trying* to be a good sport about it, but every few steps he would let out an "Oh, my God!" or a "ahahhh" with a high pitched skittishness that betrayed his gurgling stomach bile.

To be fair to Henry, as a guy who nearly craps himself when he rides the Ferris Wheel at the county fair, it wasn't like I was exactly *comfortable* with the height and its accompanying promise of death at a misstep, but the wonder of what I was seeing pushed me past my fear.

Save for an elderly couple, the top of the Rock was clear when the five of us summited. We were there. The mountaintop. No more steps to climb. Nothing around us but the wide-open sky. We gathered together, our legs burning, and smiled into the sun as the couple snapped our picture.

AT 275 feet tall and 36 feet in diameter, the General Sherman Tree is believed to be the largest tree by volume on planet Earth. As such, this tree is rightfully one of the premier attractions in all of central California. We ate our lunches on our way to see it, and it's a good thing we did because it took us about thirty minutes to find a parking spot in the lot adjacent to the paved head of the Congress Trail. This was annoying, but would have been made more so had it been amplified by hunger.

The fact that humans come from miles around just to stand at the foot of a tree, get their picture taken by it, and maybe read up on some of the neat information written on the plaques along the trail is, taken on the whole, pretty encouraging. It's good that people care about trees. That said, there is a bit of a theme park feel to the paths that lead to The General Sherman, and I couldn't help wondering if, somewhere high above, the trees were rolling their eyes at all the silly humans scurrying about beneath them.

Don't get me wrong, we took tons of pictures there too, and it was *very* cool to stand in the shade of such a creature. But something about having to wait in line to do so sanded the edges off of some of the thrill for me.

Not so for my kids, who were universally excited at both the sight of the crowds — "Look at all the people here to see a *tree!*" and the singularity of The General's girth —"Take my picture, Dad! That is the biggest tree on earth." I happily took the pictures, but it didn't take long before I was ready to go.

Maybe it wasn't the crowd that dampened my spirits but the debt of the previous night calling to be cashed. Either way, I was tired for sure, and ready to be showered and off of my feet. But we had an hour drive ahead of us before we reached the Grant Grove cabins in Kings Canyon National Park. Miles to go before I sleep, indeed.

CALL me old school, but there are few things that say, "going soft" better than the notion of "glamping." That's Glamour and Camping smashed together, for those who, like me prior to doing research for this trip, have never heard of such a thing. I like to think I live with my feet firmly on the ground and one of the things that shows that is my belief, in most cases, that that's where you should sleep if you're out in the woods. Now, don't get me wrong, I've got nothing against being comfortable, I'm just put off by images of people in chunky heels and designer clothes sipping flutes of champagne by the fire pit in front of a platform tent in which rests a queen-sized bed replete with high thread-count sheets. Why don't you just stay in a hotel for God's sake?

So it was with some trepidation that I pulled into the lot next to the John Muir Lodge in Kings Canyon. The website described the place as the "pinnacle of Kings Canyon lodging"; a few paragraphs later, wireless internet access was mentioned — both sure warning signs of a glamping vibe. Still, as I planned the trip I figured at the halfway point of our adventure, we might benefit from some of the comforts of home, which proved to be true, especially after our night in Sequoia. But there were certain lines I wasn't going to cross. I allowed that sleeping in a real bed might be acceptable provided that bed was housed in a *cabin* and there wasn't a hot tub in sight. So the John Muir Lodge was out, but a cabin in Grant Grove was in.

Just down the road from the Lodge, the cabins, each adorned with a front porch and equipped with an outdoor wood-burning stove, are clustered in a mostly wooded campground, walking distance away from a shower house that has a trough-style sink out back where you can wash your camp dishes. The shower house is nothing special. You have to use a lodge-issued token to operate the showers. Each token gives you seven minutes of water time, and you are only allowed one token per day, per person. But the stalls are private and the water runs hot, or at least warm, after the first minute or so.

God bless the angel who upon listening to my crazy story from the night before, and verifying it by glancing out her window to see my children climbing on the roof of the Sequoia and hitting each other with sticks while Theresa sat in the front seat with her head in her hands waiting for me to finish checking in, passed me an extra handful of shower tokens with a knowing wink.

See, Henry, sometimes it does pay to strike up conversations with strangers.

By the time everyone was cleaned-up and back at the cabin, the sun was on its way to setting and a chill was dancing through the air. We pulled our chairs around the fire and dug out our s'mores supplies.

When the kids were really little, I used to put them to bed at night by playing a story game I invented called "Give Me Three Things." The way it works is that whomever I am tucking in gives me three, preferably random and unrelated things: a bowl of chocolate ice cream, a magic dragonfly wing, and a pair of patched corduroy pants on the side of a country road, and it's up to me to make up a story that includes all of them. It was one of my favorite things to do as a young dad. I still remember fighting back tears the first time Henry said, "No, Dad, I'd rather read by myself," when I asked him if he wanted to play.

But there around the fire, with beds inside our cozy, non-glamping cabin waiting for us, we traveled back in time and spent the last hour of our day taking turns telling "Give Me Three Things" stories around the fire, each one sillier than the last. I could swear the trees were listening.

I guess if you ignore the "What about mes?" long enough, eventually you get your answer. Eventually you get what you need.

Threshold
(Day 11. Kings Canyon — Yosemite)

WHEN I AWOKE IN OUR cabin near Grant Grove in Kings Canyon, I felt well rested for the first time in days. I got up and built a fire. Soon Theresa and the kids were up too. As I alternated between packing up our things and tending the fire, Theresa focused on making breakfast, while Henry, Max and Harper scurried off to climb the rocky hillside behind the nearest cluster of cabins. For a while we could hear their shouts and laughter, but soon their voices faded in the distance and all was quiet.

Before they left, I told Henry he was in charge of the others and that he ought to circle back when they got hungry. Theresa and I talked about our planned morning hike in Grant Grove and the subsequent long drive to Yosemite ahead, but even as I savored our time alone together, I found my mind drifting every few minutes or so, to the uncertainty of the kids' whereabouts. As their fifteen minutes away stretched into a half an hour, I began regretting that my morning boundaries hadn't been more specific.

I was just about to sheepishly admit to Theresa that I hadn't really been listening to her, when Henry rounded the corner of the cabin with his brother and sister in tow. "Hey guys, what's for breakfast?" he asked. Just like it was any other day.

After we finished packing, we drove to Grant Grove, another cluster of Sequoias known for being home to one of the world's largest trees. In this case, The General Grant Tree named in 1867 after the Civil War hero and dubbed "The Nation's Christmas Tree" in 1926 by Calvin Coolidge (of all people).

The General Grant is nearly 1,700 years old, but at 267 some feet tall and nearly 29 feet in diameter it is, alas, not *quite* as big nor old as The General Sherman Tree — an odd fact, I thought, considering the men the trees are named after. After all, it's Ulysses S. Grant who appears on the fifty, not Sherman, the red-whiskered slasher who tore up the southern railroad lines on his historic march through Georgia, pouring salt on the Rebel's fields as he went. Wouldn't you think the bigger tree would be named after the bigger general? Anyway, who knows what the tree-namers were thinking? Either way, I blush at the arrogance that saw fit to try to measure the worth of these trees in human terms. Meters and years. Presidents and Generals.

In my experience, The General Sherman Tree and The General Grant are *both* objectively awesome and breathtaking and all the other clichés you can think of when considering whether or not Trip Advisor should deem the destination, "Worth Your Effort." But as we strolled through the fallen trunks and paved shade of Grant Grove, I couldn't help noticing the place was far less muddled with muggles than the space around The General Sherman where we had walked just the day before. Is it possible that people are so shallow that they are more likely to plan a trip to visit the world's largest tree than they are to visit the *second* largest?

Now I don't want to come off as ungrateful. I get that humans have done some pretty amazing things over the years. Abstract thought and the gifts that come with it are nothing to scoff at.

And I'll concede that, on the wonder scale, humans score pretty high. But it's also true there is nothing on this planet more selfish, nothing with a greater capacity for destruction, than a single human being.

Compare that to the Giant Sequoia, a species whose fight for survival and dominance naturally empowers a vast array of other species to thrive as well. Plus, you never have to worry about an angry Sequoia getting his nose bent out of joint over some imaginary line on a map and then launching a weapon that ends the world.

We are nothing compared to these trees.

I took one more shot of the kids, arms slung over each other's shoulders, sitting on a split-rail fence with a cluster of trunks, each of which would barely fit in our backyard, standing tall behind them. Then I put my phone back in my pocket and headed to the car. No need to check the latest provocation on Twitter today. I have it on good faith from a couple of generals that all that nonsense will be over soon enough.

EVER since Henry was very little, he's suffered from periodic migraine headaches. For a while, before we knew what was really going on, it was pretty scary. He'd get this look in his eyes and that would be *it* for the day. Just a lot of crying, screaming, and barfing. And then he'd pass out dead. Like check his pulse and breathing, dead. And he'd have to sleep it off until the next morning.

We took him to all sorts of doctors and neurological centers, but their conclusions were never that helpful. *Some kids grow out of it. Managing the pain is really the best thing you can do. There's this experimental drug that might help take the edge off; now let's talk about the side effects.* I just wanted my kid to feel better.

Now that he's older, Henry can mostly manage the headaches, which aren't nearly as common or severe as they used to be, on his own. If one sets in, he'll usually duck into the bathroom to vomit, then take a shower and curl up in his bed in the dark for an hour or so until the worst of it passes.

None of these options, of course, were available to him on the side of Route 41, but that didn't stop Henry's migraine from coming on strong two hours into our four-hour drive from Grant Grove to Yosemite Lake RV resort, where we planned to pitch our tent for the next few days. By the time we pulled into Coarsegold, on our way to Mariposa Grove, Henry had hurled into garbage cans at three separate gas stations. Coarsegold was our fourth stop.

"That's a shit ton of Gatorade, man."

I took one look at the woman behind the counter: tattoos, wrinkled skin a shade somewhere between red and brown that you can't find in a Crayola box, a break-cigarette holding her hair back behind her ear, and decided I could trust her. "Yeah, my kid's got a migraine. He's been puking for over an hour. Just trying to keep him hydrated until we get to the park."

"Yosemite?"

"Yeah, we're out here from Buffalo. So we're heading into Mariposa Grove to see where the butterflies visit, then we'll do the whole, drive-through the tree thing before heading through the park to our campground."

"Where are you camping?" she asked. If she didn't care about the growing line of customers behind me then neither did I.

"An RV park my wife and I read about online. We don't have an RV though. We're tenting."

"With a puking kid? Shit, good luck with *that*."

"Well, here's hoping these'll help him stop." I pushed the Gatorades across the counter and took out my wallet to pay, but the guy behind me grabbed my arm. I flinched away and turned to face him.

"I just came from that way," he said, his palms up to show he wasn't after my cash. "They're doing road work up there. The traffic is backed up for, like, an hour both ways. I'm just sayin, you go that way, you won't be getting to any campsite in the north part of the park any time before dark. No way."

With the memory of our Hard Good night in Sequoia etched firmly in my brain, I asked, "Is there another way into Yosemite? A way that'll avoid the back-up?" Three people in line pulled out their phones and started pecking away to help.

"Look at this, Buffalo." The cashier pulled out a greasy map from under the register and pushed my Gatorades aside so she could spread it out. Her finger traced a route around the western side of the park that cut in near our campground. "Take this and you'll miss the mess this guy's talking about. It's *longer* in miles, but you'll be moving the whole time. No one hardly goes that way."

I looked at the guy behind me who shrugged, "That'll work," he said. "No traffic that way for sure."

When I got back to the car I spread out our map and drew a penciled line along the route the cashier showed me. "It means missing the drive-through-tree and seeing where the butterflies go, but we'll get to the campsite before dark this way."

"Whatever gets us there faster," Henry said around the open mouth of his Gatorade bottle. "I'm dying here." Max and Harper sat looking out their respective windows. Neither of them said a word.

My fourth grade teacher, Mr. Gard changed the trajectory of my life. Not because every day after lunch he read our class great books like, *Where the Red Fern Grows* and *The Search for Delicious*. Not because the way he taught American history made it feel so much like a cool story that I once sneaked out of lunch early so I could beat my classmates to the library and check out a biography of Stonewall Jackson. And not because he let us watch the TV (rolled in on a special cart just for the occasion) for an hour after the space shuttle *Challenger*, with teacher Christa McAuliffe on board, blew up right before our eyes. All of the other teachers in the grade switched their TVs off, but Mr. Gard knew better. We'd been studying space travel for weeks. It's not like we didn't know death was a possibility. Instead of shielding us from it, he felt it with us. We weren't fourth grade kids that day; we were humans. Just like him. No, the thing I'm most grateful to Mr. Gard for, the lesson I'm sure I'll remember for as long as I live, is the one he taught us about butterflies.

I can still see the rectangular screened-in habitat he kept near the front of the room. Housed inside was a full milkweed plant in a quart mason jar for the yellow, black, and white striped caterpillar who, to my untrained eyes, looked like a fat worm dressed up for Halloween.

Eventually, after the plant was twice replaced, its leaves nibbled down to nothing, the creature crawled to the top of the cage and hung itself in a stiff J. The next morning, the J was replaced by a glowing green oval (the shade of which I'd never seen before), bedazzled with a cluster of golden pin points near the top; a chrysalis, Mr. Gard explained.

Each day we returned to school anxious to see what was next in the caterpillar's transformative process. Slowly the green darkened. Soon the chrysalis turned black, and we all assumed tragedy. We dutifully sketched the image of hanging death in our field notebooks, only to find the next day that, out of the darkness, an outline of the familiar orange and black wings of a Monarch appeared, as if shrink-wrapped inside the now-clear casing of the chrysalis.

We came back from recreation that day to find Mr. Gard, breathless. His eyes danced and glistened and he gathered us on the ground around the cage to get a better look at the butterfly who clung with brittle legs to the side of the screen, pumping his wings full before our astonished eyes.

For a week after, Mr. Gard let us observe the Monarch. We took turns feeding it nectar from a shallow dish, wrote poems in tribute to its first flight around the cage, and ardently argued about what we ought to name it; a conundrum with no conclusion, for Mr. Gard refused to settle the matter for us.

Then one bright, early autumn day, we let the butterfly go.

Parents came to school to watch the release. Then the whole group went back to the classroom to circle around our desks and take in the displays we created celebrating what we learned about Monarchs.

As I stood by my diorama, I remember hearing a man mutter to his wife, "All this fuss over a bug!"

My eyes instantly filled with angry tears, but then a girl named Whitney, whose desk was next to mine, grabbed my hand and whispered, "Don't worry, Matthew. He just doesn't understand." And it was true. It was as if we were all in on this amazing secret. All of us kids and this magician of a teacher, Mr. Gard. We knew what the others didn't: those orange and black specs floating above the fall fields of western New York weren't *bugs*; they were *miracles*.

Every year since fourth grade, I've caught a monarch caterpillar so I could watch it make its journey back to the wind. By late September, you could find me standing on the edge of a cornfield somewhere, or knee deep in the buzzing weeds near the gravel road that leads to our cottage by the lake, or on the grassy hill across from my grandma's house, even once behind my freshman dorm in a furtive moment of freedom between football practices — an empty jar held in my outstretched hand, watching the flight of an orange and black miracle released to the wind.

If I had to sum up my faith in a phrase it would be this: the caterpillar's death is the butterfly's beginning. Amen and amen.

YOSEMITE Park sits squarely in the migratory path of the Western Monarch. Each summer, as the weather begins to cool, they make their way south toward Santa Cruz and San Diego, where they spend the winter darting through the temperate breezes before heading north again to breed. As such, on early August days, a hiker in the southern part of Yosemite National Park is likely to see groves of trees swarming with butterflies.

But the annual count of Monarchs, regularly in the millions throughout the 1980s, is down nearly 90%. Deforestation. Pesticides. Human sprawl. A warming and drying climate. All of these factors assure that what was once inconceivable, now seems all but certain. My children's children will never know the sight of a live Monarch butterfly.

I had planned our swing through southern Yosemite with the hope that the sight of the butterflies on the branches would be beautiful enough to etch an image in my children's minds that would last at least another generation. Maybe Harper would write a poem about it. Maybe Henry would sketch a picture to hang on our refrigerator door. Maybe someday Max would tell his sons about the time he stood in the forest with his family and saw the branches alive and dripping with life as if dipped in an orange and black honey.

But maybe it's already too late.

I turned on the car and pointed it toward the mountain road that led around the park toward our campground in the northern part of Yosemite. "We'll skip the butterflies this time around, okay guys?" I said with more assurance than I felt. I looked in the rearview mirror, then said, "Hold on, Henry. We'll be there soon."

THERESA grew up taking trips down to Virginia in her family's camper, so she holds a decidedly romantic view of RV culture. Whereas I tend to see RVs more through the windshield of a driver who has been stuck behind one too many gas-guzzling house-buses chugging their way slowly up and down the rolling hills of Central New York toward a glorified grassy parking lot where they'll rest for the night with other such behemoths plugged into an outlet and hooked-up to a sewage chute so the driver can truly enjoy the natural wonders of "camping."

Still, I've heard it said that the secret of a long marriage is mastering the art of compromise. Which is why, on the eve of our eighteenth wedding anniversary, Theresa and I pulled into Yosemite Lakes RV campground with three exhausted children, a stinking bag of sticky laundry, and a shared desire to be done with the day on our minds. All I cared about at that point was the park's laundry facilities, the promise of live local music later on, and the smell of warm tacos wafting up from under a broad and shady tent. "Enjoy the place," the lady at the registration desk said.

"Will do," I smiled back. Then I ushered Henry out the door and around the back of the building where we found an old oil drum garbage can, which Henry used to great effect in an effort to finally rid his loins of the last of his Gatorade.

"Let's go set up the tent, buddy. Mom can stay down here with Harper and Max. She's got to take care of the laundry anyhow and I'm sure you're in no mood to eat."

"I'm actually starving, Dad," Henry said, whipping the vomit off his face with the back of his wrist. "Plus, I feel fine."

"Looks like it."

"Dad, *please.*"

"No! You've been barfing for the last two hours."

"That's *why* I'm hungry," Henry insisted.

"Absolutely not. I don't want to spend another night roaming around a campground with a puking child."

"C'mon, Dad! I'm *fine.* And besides, this seems like it'll be fun." It was his last statement that convinced me.

The band playing that night was a group of silverback gorillas: dudes somewhere between my age and the age of my parents. Their promo poster made me think of the band equipment I slept next to in Santa Barbara. They call themselves *Threshold* and are described as a horn band specializing in 60s and 70s music. In other words, *exactly* the type of sound I spent the first ten years of Henry's life trying to indoctrinate him into. But you can list my attempt to give Henry good taste in music as Dad Fail #2,768 because these days the boy who once happily sang along to the likes of The Eagles, The Allman Brothers and Bob Dylan now happily lists five different rappers with the first name of, *Lil* as his favorite artists. Yet here he was, showing some openness to the joy of good live music. How could I say no?

"I'll make a deal with you," I said. "You help Mom get the laundry started and go back with her to switch it to the dryer when it's time — without a single complaint — and I'll go get the food with Harper and Max. When you guys are done you can join us." Henry stuck out his hand in an oddly formal gesture and we shook on it like men.

THE campsites, though kind of carved into the hillside, were mostly flat and pretty tightly packed. The best one we could find was nestled less than fifteen feet from a small cabin. Once we set up the tent, we drove back down the hill with stomachs rumbling, just in time to jump in line for truck tacos as the band began to play.

Max helped me pull a picnic table into the shady corner close to the makeshift stage. Together we gathered the family orders, paid the vendor, and set the food out while Henry and Harper helped Theresa load the laundry.

The kids scarfed down their meals in less than five minutes and ran off to celebrate National S'mores Day by toasting marshmallows with the horde of other chocolate-smeared kids now gathered around the community fire pit — stacked high with flaming pallets. There Theresa and I were: alone at last.

Ah, *alone at last.*

Are there three other words strung together in the English language that better characterize the challenge that is being married with kids? Many days, Theresa and I are lucky to have twenty minutes to ourselves. And when we do get them, those twenty minutes are often spent going over schedules, planning events, or hashing out the best way to address a kid who sneaked out of the backyard during a sleepover to go swimming out of bounds in the community pool at 2:00 a.m.. It's nice to have an Assistant

Manager, but sometimes I miss my wife even though we sleep in the same bed every night.

When you're married with kids, spending time alone with your spouse always feels like a transaction — giving one thing up in exchange for another. It's almost never pure. The way it works for us is we both wake up really early and talk over breakfast or we plug the kids into the electronic babysitter in the evening so we can retire to the front room of our pretty-small house to compare notes on the day. Now that the kids are older, we can take walks together too, but I often find a nagging feeling of leaving the kids behind is walking along with us wherever we go.

And when you're strung out from the day with no time together to recharge, cracks form in the bedrock of your relationship. Rather than seeing the woman sitting across from you at dinner as this beautiful, soulful angel who changed your life by seeing both the best and worst in you and loving you anyway, you see someone who's too damn busy looking at her phone for two hours every day to dust the damn mantle like she said she would three separate times last week. Instead of asking yourself, what can I do to show her how much I love and appreciate her, you ask yourself, How fucking hard is it to dust a mantle? You could do it yourself, of course, it's not like dusting the mantle is *difficult* — I mean that's kind of the point. It's just that you've been at work all day and she's been at home after getting the kids off to school. Isn't shit like dusting the mantle her job?

Soon, instead of looking at your spouse through wedding-day glasses, and giving her the benefit of the doubt, you end up doing just the opposite. And then you're just pissed off all the time. When "alone at last" finally comes, you end up fighting over stupid shit like who left the top off the peanut butter jar, which is definitely annoying, but also, really not worth *fighting* about. But when "alone at last" only happens every once in a while, *everything* feels like it's something major.

I sang along to nearly every song as Theresa and I sat next to each other, our hands casually clasped together, alternating our gaze between the band and the s'mores-stick fencing match our sons were having with a group of shaggy blonde boys they'd met by the fire. Harper wasn't too far away either. She busied herself jumping from rock to rock over a triangle of boulders set to mark the boundary of the grandstand, shouting out instructions to her brothers as she went.

When the first set was over, Theresa got up to get the laundry. "Don't forget to grab Henry," I said. "He promised he would help."

"He's having fun, Matt. Just let it go. I got this."

Theresa has the prettiest hazel eyes. Green with slices of brown, rimmed with an outline of unearthly blue. I've never seen anything like them. It was one of the first things I noticed about her. That and her gorgeous smile. Plus, she's got this easy laugh that makes her nose crinkle up in the cutest way. And she's smart and funny. She sees things I don't see. Makes me care about stuff I otherwise would ignore. She's everything I want to be. She makes me better.

I used to make Theresa mixtapes all the time, and *Brown-Eyed Girl* was one of my go-to songs. I picked *Brown-Eyed Girl* only because nobody ever wrote a song about a girl with eyes like Theresa's. There have never been eyes like Theresa's.

When I saw that she'd gone into the campground's laundry facility, I went over to the lead singer of the band and asked if they could play *Brown-Eyed Girl* for me in the next set.

I explained we were out from the Buffalo area, camping with

our kids, and that tomorrow was our wedding anniversary. The lead singer was a big guy. Sunglasses. Goatee. Great range. The type of guy who when you hear him sing you can't help thinking, *"What's he doing in an RV park on a Saturday night?"* He just kind of stared at me for a beat when I asked about the song. Then the lead guitarist came over.

"Hey man, you've been singing along to everything." He stuck out his hand, "I'm Steve." Steve wore a Hawaiian shirt, ratty jeans, a baseball cap and sunglasses. I once saw Paul Simon perform in exactly the same outfit.

I introduced myself and then said, "I love your stuff. You guys can really jam." Steve's face split into a grin. "My wife and I are out here from Buffalo camping with our kids, and tomorrow's our eighteenth wedding anniversary. Any chance you can play *Brown-Eyed Girl* for us?"

"We'll get it in the next set for sure," Steve said. "Right, Mike?" But before Goatee and Sunglasses could answer, Steve clapped me on the shoulder like he'd known me his entire life. "Camping with the kids for your anniversary, huh? That's great."

When I returned to the picnic table I found Henry, Max and Harper full of questions. Henry, who is embarrassed by anything I do, was the lead prosecutor.

"Why were you talking to those guys, Dad? Is something wrong?"

"No nothing's wrong. It's a surprise."

"Where's Mom?"

"She's off *by herself* finishing the laundry," I said.

"I didn't know, okay? We were fencing!" Henry replied, instantly defensive. "Sorry for having fun. God!"

"Relax, dude. I just . . . "

"Mommy!" Harper shrieked and streaked away toward Theresa, who, having stored our now folded clothes in the trunk of the car, was making her way back to us.

"Just be cool, Henry, okay. Can you be cool?"

"I'll be cool, Dad," Max said, stuffing his mouth full of a melty chocolate bar he'd been saving for later. "What's going on?"

"Yeah, what's going on?" Theresa asked slightly out of breath. But before I could answer, Morrison's opening chords announced the beginning of the next set.

I pulled Theresa out onto the grassy area in front of the stage. I can't remember the last time I danced. I felt slow and awkward and silly, but Theresa was laughing, the crowd started clapping, and soon two other women joined us on the "dance floor." Another family pushed their table back to make room. By the end of the song, a crowd was forming in front of the stage. Happy Anniversary.

Threshold — From left to right: Steve Preston, John de Jonge, Martin Martinez, Mike Collins, and Dave Monday (not pictured, Ronnie Meyer on drums). National S'mores Day. Yosemite Lakes RV Campground. Groveland, California.

THE band was still playing an hour later as we walked back together toward the car. The kids were chattering to each other about their favorite songs. Henry liked the Motown stuff. Harper liked when we danced. Max couldn't stop talking about how Steve climbed onto our picnic table and jammed a solo before jumping into a mid-air split and sprinting back to the stage.

Theresa was mostly quiet, but as we fell in step with each other behind the kids, she slipped her arm around me and leaned her head against my shoulder. It was almost dark.

Our wedding day. The birth of our kids. The recovery room after the miscarriage. The night the call came about Theresa's mom. Thresholds every one. Each a portal that marked the end of one time and the beginning of another.

In a long life together, it's natural to look at time this way. Certain pages of the photo album see more light than others. You remember The Moments and the rest just fades to noise. The hanging J, the chrysalis, that first dunking and dipping flight. But there is more to raising a butterfly than that. Love is the lesson.

Every day a door opens to a new way of being. There's a chance to begin again. We walked together arm-in-arm as the sun set over the mountains. A lifetime of memories swirling through my head.

The Promises
(Day 12. Yosemite)

Everything I read about Yosemite warned of its distinctive theme park feel: big crowds, thick lines, and not enough parking spaces. Usually, these types of descriptors scare me off, but considering Yosemite is the subject of nearly every damn Ansell Adams picture I've ever seen, it seemed worth the hassle. So we shook the kids awake with the sun and hustled through our morning at camp hoping to beat the hordes.

Soon we were buzzing past El Capitan on our way to Yosemite Village where we planned to park for the day. Theresa spread a park map across the dashboard and pointed out spots where we might stop. Soon she found a hardly marked trail leading toward Sentinel Beach, a tucked away picnic grove on the banks of the Merced River.

We walked along the trail in a single-file line through alternating expanses of dense underbrush and airy pines. When the woods fell away and the yawning valley opened up before us, none of us could move. Towering rock faces cut jagged edges into the sunlit sky. An impossibly blue backdrop framed the timeworn foothills. No one spoke. Then, as if in a shared trance, we walked again, drawn toward the river, which flowed smooth and slow in the slanting morning sun.

On the banks of the Merced, Harper slipped off her shoes and waded in to her ankles. She stood with the sun in her hair looking at the surrounding stone. Max went further, as is his nature, past his knees. Rolling his shorts high, he stood nearly in the middle of the flow, looking for fish with the keen eyes of a hunter. I found Henry around a slight bend, laying sprawled out in the sun, two warm stones placed over his eyes as if coins for Charon's collection on the other side of Lethe.

I don't know how this world began or if, rather than beginning, it always just was. Maybe the truth of creation's birth pains must be forgotten. The transition from darkness to light so terrible that the only way to bear it is to hide from its wonder in stories of creatures brought forth out of water and clay. But if someone said for certain that this was the place. This valley. This river. This morning. This Holy Now. This is where it all began and begins and forever will flow — I would believe it.

BOB Dylan had it right when he wrote, *"It's easy to see without looking too far / that not much is really sacred."* And I was singing that song as we made our way through Yosemite Village, the park's capital of consumerism where seemingly everything, from the practical to the purposeless, is for sale. I sometimes think if given the chance, humans would set up a souvenir shop outside of the gates of heaven. FOR SALE: T-shirts embossed with God's face over some witty phrase about sin and salvation, insulated travel mugs that change color when you think of your best day on earth, and little plastic keychain tubes filled with strands of "angel hair" promised to belong to the spirits of your long lost loved ones.

The juxtaposition of the jam packed parking lot and overpriced kitsch of the village with the striking vistas all around us was so mind-bending it created a kind of surreal clarity. There have been times in my life when I've *really* wanted something like a t-shirt or a mug. But the Sentinel Beach-Village Gift Shop sequence taught me otherwise once and for all. The gifts of the world can't be bought in a store.

AT some 2,425 feet above the valley floor, Yosemite Falls is the tallest waterfall in North America. There's a trail that snakes along the entire length of it, but it takes an average hiker six-to-eight hours to walk. The kids were already showing signs of wear and it was barely ten in the morning, so instead of tackling the entire trail, we made our way from the Visitor's Center to the shuttle stop where a wide paved path leads to the still-pretty-awesome-at-320 feet, Lower Falls.

We jostled through the dense crowd to the base. A jumble of house-sized boulders stood on the other side of the wooden viewing deck. Signs posted everywhere warned of imminent injuries, dismemberment and death if one was foolish enough to climb onto the sometimes-slick boulders for a better view.

But, diminished as it was, the mid-August flow of the waterfall left large sections of the rocks mostly dry, exposing open and well-worn paths that twisted toward the falls around deep pools, flowing rivulets and swirling eddies. The whispered invitation was too good to ignore, so against Theresa's better judgment, we looked past the signs and began to climb the rocks, seeking a closer connection to the water that plunged to the valley floor from heights above.

Henry and Max scrambled forward at a frantic rate, while Theresa and Harper lagged behind, carefully negotiating the crags and gullies. I was torn in the middle, wanting to keep pace with the boys, to guide them and push back against their foolish impulses, and at the same time feeling the pressing need to be a hand for Harper to hold as she jumped from rock to rock.

"Boys! You've got to wait for us. We'll be right there."

"But I see a route right ahead, Dad! We'll scout it out."

"Henry, stop! Wait for Mom and Harper."

"Why don't *you* wait for them? We'll go ahead and find a good spot to rest."

"I need to be able to see you. What if you fell? What if Max falls?"

"We're not going to fall. Why did you bring us here if you aren't going to let us try to do it?"

"Just *wait* damn it!

On a cold January morning in 2013, I lost track of three-year-old Max at an over-crowded Sectional wrestling meet. One second he was holding my hand, the next second he was gone. In the time between when I realized he was missing and when the teenage girl who found him brought him back to me — his face red with tears, his shirt soaked with sweat — my mind was a fast-forward slide show of terror. Though he wasn't missing for more than ten minutes, those remain some of the ripest moments of fear I have ever experienced. Primal, complete and devastating. Like when you jerk awake from a dream in which you're falling into the open air and there's nothing you can do to save yourself. Only it was much worse than that, because it wasn't *my* survival I was worried about. I was worried about my kid.

"DAD, come on! We'll be fine. I'm thirt*een*."

"Okay," I said. "I'll be here with Mom and Harper if you need me." Henry nodded, but didn't say a word. "Look after your brother," I said after him. "And hurry back." But the boys were already gone. Scurrying up the face of a boulder, they disappeared over the other side into the roaring mist of the falls.

A handful of minutes passed before Theresa and Harper caught up to me. When they slid down the smooth face of a rock-chunk the size of our garage, Harper jumped into my arms. Theresa looked around, a bit out of breath, a growing sense of urgency in her manner. "Where are the boys?" she said with an I-can't-be-lieve-I-have-to-ask-this-question laugh.

"I let them go ahead," I said. "Henry saw a path that would take us up closer to the bottom of the falls."

"You just let them go?"

"I wanted to give them a chance to try it on their own? Don't worry," I reassured her, "They've only been gone a few minutes. Henry promised he would circle back and get us." But even as those words came out of my mouth, I knew they were a lie. Henry made no such promise.

THE first time I saw Henry, he was grayish white and hanging upside down, his slippery feet in the left hand of Dr. Leonard Mirada, whose other hand was smacking Henry's naked behind in an attempt to make him breath. There was no first cry of life, no joyful moment of the baby on his mother's breast, no picture of me holding my son. Instead there was a team of nurses rushing in, the blood-soaked hospital floor, and the ride up the freight elevator with the nurse who said, "Your son is very sick. We want you to see him properly. Tell him his name. It's likely he won't make it. When we go back downstairs, it'll be your job to tell your wife." And then the elevator doors flew open and the neon lights of the neonatal intensive care unit blinded me.

But Henry survived. A month later we brought him home on oxygen. He slept with a monitor glued to his chest, a nasal cannula up his nostrils feeding his lungs the sweet air he needed to thrive.

Almost a year later, Theresa went to visit a friend in Rochester and left me home alone with Henry for the first time. I fed him cut up cantaloupe by the handful in his high chair. When he began to turn blue, I delivered back blows, his head between my knees, until the piece of fruit stuck in his throat broke free and came spilling out onto our front steps.

I taught him how to throw a baseball, taped his crayon drawings up next to our wedding picture in the living room, and ran around our yard in circles pushing him in a wheelbarrow, while he squealed in delight.

The promises made between a father and child are often unspoken. I will love you. I will give you my life. Anything. And in return all I ask is that you don't waste it. Be brave. Hold fast to what I taught you. Never forget our stories.

But eventually the child climbs over the rocks and out of sight and you are left in the silence, hoping he will make it back to you. Hoping he will remember the promises.

"Mom! Dad! You've got to see this! Max is waiting." Henry came back.

Theresa, Harper and I followed as he led us through a series of shoulder-width trails squeezed between the stones. The falls roared behind us from on high. At last we saw Max sitting by himself in the sun. His feet dangled over an edge that hovered above a knee-deep pool fed on all sides by broken streams from the mountain. We stayed there together, in the spot the boys found, for over an hour. Sometimes silent. Sometimes laughing. Sometimes dipping our feet in the pool. Henry and Max beamed with pride. "Can you believe we found this spot, Dad?" Henry said. "I told you we would be okay."

"Yes, buddy. I should have trusted you," I smiled back.

"I got this," he said. "Trust the process." Then he looked away out over the vast horizon of mountains and trees and water.

"I'll remember next time," I said. Another promise.

After a quick lunch of bagged chicken, granola bars and fruit (it's amazing what passes for edible when you're on the road), we hopped back onto a shuttle headed for a hike to Mirror Lake.

Mirror Lake is formed by the snowmelt waters of Tenaya Creek that gather in between Half Dome and North Dome—two hulking masses of iconic rock that punch their way toward the sky from the valley floor. When the water's surface is still in the spring and early summer, it reflects the surrounding sky to stunning effect. But each year, by late August, an early autumn meadow emerges.

Flowers and grass replacing the placid flow now swallowed by the earth until the spring's sun Easters it back into being.

We hiked the looped-trail together. And when we came into the clearing we found that though the previous winter was brief, the spring rains infrequent, and the summer somewhat dry, the promised blessing of Mirror Lake's shimmering surface remained palpably present in the mid-August sun.

In the sheltered shade of a grove of birches, the boys and I stripped to our shorts and ditched our shoes before diving into the cool waters. We swam together, with earnest strokes, toward a huge rock that seemed to float on the surface of the deepest part of the lake.

With clinging toes, we found footholds and clutched our way up the smooth, slick sundrenched surface of the boulder island, until we stood together on its narrow zenith. Wonder surrounded us on all sides. We floated there together, as if in the palm of God's hand, our laughter and shouts swallowed by the open blue of the heavens.

"Dad, we've got to jump in!" Max's eyes shown toward me, his body, like an otter's — all muscle, dripping wet.

"I'm not sure how deep it is, Max. And that's a good drop too." Standing with my toes curled over the edge I looked down into the rock-shaded pool.

"Are you going to jump?" Harper shouted from the shore.

"Is it deep enough, Matt?" Theresa asked.

A stranger toweling himself off on the far bank called out to us, "It's deep enough, you guys." His teenage son, standing next to him, gave us a silent thumbs up as he tossed his hair out of his face. "Just make sure to get some distance. You've got to clear the rocks around the bottom if you want to hit the deeper part of the pool." I smiled my thanks, even as I realized that his words left me with little choice but to leap.

"Okay, boys," I said. "Count to three." And on "three" I jumped.

When I hit the water I splayed my hands out to the side and braced my knees to absorb the blow of the bottom, which came surprisingly swift and soft, its mud squishing through my toes. The drop from the top of the rock to the water was long enough to notice you were in the air. Maybe twenty feet. The pool I now treaded in was half that depth at best. I looked up into the summer sun to see Max swinging his arms above me, readying himself to fly.

"Max! Wait! You've got to clear the rocks. It's not as deep as it looks."

"Will you stay there, Dad? Just in case I need you?" I nodded.

"Okay, buddy. I'm ready when you are. I'll count for you." Max jumped on three and disappeared below the surface of the clear water with amazing speed. But his head burst up with a radiant smile, and before I could get to him, he turned to his brother who stood waiting, half-hunched on top of the rock.

"C'mon, Henry! It's awesome!"

I held off Henry long enough to swim Max safely to shore, where Theresa and Harper waited for him. Then I swam back out and treaded water in the shade beneath Henry, counting down at a safe distance before he too leapt into the air toward me.

By the time Henry and I crawled out onto the rocky shore, Max was already knee-deep in the water, anxious to try again. "I'll go again too," Henry said, a broad smile on his face. "You should video us, Mom. This is epic. Let's go, Dad." The boys knew better than to ask Theresa to jump.

"I want to try," Harper said. Standing next to Theresa, she suddenly seemed impossibly small. She wore an olive green shirt with a bunny on it. Her hair was pulled back into a ponytail, but blonde wisps twisted free and blew across her face as she looked up at me with determined eyes. "I can do it."

"Harper, you don't have a bathing suit," Theresa reminded her. "Plus that's a long swim and a big drop." Theresa smiled down at her in a way that made her unspoken "No," seem final.

"The boys got to jump, Mom!"

"The boys aren't seven, sweetheart. I just think it's a little too much."

"Theresa, can I talk to you a minute?" We walked a few paces to the side. Once out of earshot I said, "Theresa, think of the message we're sending to her if we don't let her do this. I know it seems like too much, but I think we've *got* to let her try."

"Matt, she doesn't have a bathing suit."

"So she'll go in her underwear. I'll swim her out. I won't let anything happen to her, sweetheart. I *promise*." Theresa looked back at me from underneath the shade of her hat, a small smile tracing her lips.

WHEN she was a junior in college, Theresa studied in Australia for a semester. I was out of school and working at Williston Northampton. Late in the term, Theresa wrote that she and some friends were planning to use the last week of the trip to do some adventuring.

"Adventuring" in this case meant skydiving over Queensland, and bungee jumping in New Zealand. Theresa, however, feared she might have to pass on some of the thrills as she was almost out of cash. Flush as I was with my first-year-teacher salary, I wired her what she needed the next day. The way I figured it, a girl doesn't often get the chance to jump out of a plane.

THE boys and I swam Harper out to the rock. She used my back and head as a ladder out of the water and Max helped pull her up the rest of the way to the top. Once I was in, Harper stood on the edge with her brothers looking down at my floating form in the water below.

"Count to three," she said. And when I did, she threw her arms out before her, her feet dancing in the air all the way down.

I am sure that when the sun sets on my lifetime, I won't remember the look of awe on the other girl's face, standing on the shore with her mother and father, when Harper and I climbed out on the bank soaking wet and laughing together after jumping off the rock. "I want to jump too, Daddy," the other little girl said.

Just as I am sure I won't remember the long walk back to the car after taking a wrong turn on the trail and missing the shuttle stop, nor the tired drive to the campsite. The quarrelsome dinner of dehydrated mash. I won't remember the boys chopping wood, the smoky fire they started, or the ghost stories we told after dark until our speech slurred with exhaustion and we finally zipped into bed.

But as long as I live, I will see my daughter falling toward me through the open air, her mane of blonde hair lifted up on the wind. Her eyes on mine, my arms outstretched — each of us trusting the promises, both spoken and unspoken, that would see us back safely to shore.

Just As I Am
(Day 13. Yosemite — Lake Tahoe)

As the morning broke, I lay on the ground with my sleeping family just outside of Yosemite National Park, listening to, beyond all reason, the prattling dialogue of three French people. The previous night, after our latest round of fireside storytelling burnt itself out, I brought an armful of firewood over to our neighboring campsite, a small cabin built into the hill just a few feet away from where we pitched our tent. "We're leaving in the morning," I explained to the woman and teenage boy sitting by the fire. "We won't be using this wood. You guys are welcome to it if you'd like." The boy and his mother smiled back at me blankly for a moment before a fit man, a decade older than me if I had to guess, bounced down the cabin steps and strode toward me with his hand extended.

In excellent English, the father explained that his wife and son didn't really understand what I was saying. They were from Paris, touring the American West for the summer. He was a businessman who split his time between France and New York. He planned the trip because he wanted to give his seventeen-year-old son a taste of the U.S. before he left home for the university.

The next morning, I lay eavesdropping in on our neighbors' morning chatter, trying my best to piece together their French phrases. From what I could tell, just like us, they were hoping to get an early start to their day. Just like us, each of them had a role in the process of packing up camp. Just like us they were doing their best to shake off the cloak of exhaustion that comes with living out of your car and embrace the excitement of the day.

As their conversation washed over me and the sleepy morning sun's heat beat down on my side of the tent, I slipped into a dream about the summer before I went to college.

ONE day in early July, I received an official looking package in the mail with a letter and a book inside of it. The letter explained Hobart and William Smith's First Year Seminar program: students rank a list of offered classes, the colleges then assign each incoming student a section (taught by the professor who serves as their academic advisor), and clusters the students from the class together in dorms to assure that all incoming first-years are taking at least one class with a person near whom they live. The letter also explained that to facilitate campus-wide discussion and community building, every incoming first year student would read T.H. White's, *The Once and Future King*, take notes and come to the initial meeting of their First Year Seminar prepared to talk about the book, regardless of the otherwise noted subject of the course. A fiercely liberal arts approach, to be sure.

I was not a great high school student. Obsessed as I was with playing football and distracted by the turmoil of my older brother's personal unraveling and the subsequent near-demise of my parents' marriage, school often came last on my list of adolescent priorities. But the aforementioned letter and 600-plus-page book served notice that if I hoped to be successful in college I needed to step up my academic effort.

I had already been at school for two weeks, getting my butt kicked at pre-season football camp when the first morning of orientation arrived. I gathered up all 600-plus pages of my well-annotated text, along with my nearly full notebook of journal entries and left my dorm room early to walk over to my first college class.

You know how some moments in life get etched in your brain? Little details that at the time seem totally irrelevant to the experience become vivid landmarks. The trash can that took everything inside me not to throw against the wall as Theresa and I waited with a group of faceless strangers for the elevator's silver doors to open after being told our daughter was likely to die. The way my brother's hair flew across his face when my mother's open hand smashed against his teeth as he stood in the living room where we always put the Christmas tree — red-blue lights of the police car flashing across all corners of the house. The fluorescent glow that cast my shadow on the gray and maroon speckled carpet in the hallway of Theresa's dorm, as I stood with sweaty hands, hoping to end my first date with my future wife with a kiss.

How does the mind know that this is one of *those* times? How does it decide what details to gather? Are the shelves stocked in real time or are the books only put back after the library closes for the night? Imagine what would happen if we could find a way to always set our mind's seismic meters to the most sensitive setting. What would we see that we otherwise miss? Is such a way of being what it's like to truly be alive?

The sun shone as I walked to class. Clay pots full of geraniums, marigolds, purple flowers, and something white, edged the curving brick steps that faced the flushed green carpet of Hobart's sprawling central quad. Looking out, I tried to imagine a new life for myself. And just as the moment rounded toward cliché, I saw a plaque embedded in the brick. Placed in the exact same spot where, four years later, I, along with the rest of my graduating class, would clutch my ticket to the wider world.

"The Ends Pre-Exist in the Means."

There were twenty minutes before class started, so I sat down next to Emerson's words and tried to puzzle out what they meant. The results are baked into the process. Everything is connected. You can't get *There* without first fully being *Here*. The sun broke through a shadow and I saw at once the purpose for the colleges assigning us *The Once and Future King*. Each step of Arthur's journey — from The Wart to the Sword to the throne — each creature he becomes during his lessons with Merlin, all of these experiences make The Round Table possible. It is only through such a life that Arthur becomes such a King. The ends pre-exist in the means.

Proud of myself for having figured out the purpose of my college education before I even took a class, I made my way to the designated spot on the quad where my First Year Seminar group was set to meet. As we waited for Professor Thiesmeyer to arrive, I ignored the chance to engage in the awkward beginnings of friendships and instead scanned the group for any signs of *The Once and Future King*. From what I saw, I was the only person carrying a book. Finally I asked the guy next to me (deep tan, Long Island accent, perfect teeth, probably wearing a thirty dollar pair of underwear) what he thought of the book.

"I didn't read that shit," he laughed. "I threw it out the day it arrived. A thousand bucks says we don't even talk about it. They just sent it out to put a scare in us."

The girl sitting next to me spoke up, "I'm not sure if it's that bad. I brought the book with me. I didn't read it either, but worst case, if we do end up needing to talk about it, I can just read it tonight. It's only the first section."

"What do you mean, it's only the first section?" I asked.

"We just had to read *The Sword in the Stone.*"

"What? You mean I read the whole book and took notes *for nothing?*"

"Man, that's like 600 pages, right?" Long Island laughed. "Happy summer."

"Right," I said, limply holding up my dog-eared copy and tattered composition book for evidence. "Happy summer."

Professor Thiesmeyer arrived, looking as though he'd come directly from central casting, and after a brief round of introductions, he asked all of us to take out our books and notes. Given that I was the only one in the group so prepared, he broadened the conversation to address the larger themes of the text. That's when I told everyone about the plaque on the steps and the conclusions it led me to that morning.

"I guess that's why we were assigned the book, right? It's the school's way of trying to remind us, or teach us maybe, what our college education is all about. Just like Arthur, every step of our journey matters."

"That's so cliché, dude." Even though he hadn't read the book, Long Island wanted to push back against my idea. "Every middle school classroom has that poster on its walls: *Shoot for the moon! Even if you miss you'll still end up in the stars.* Come on!"

"Now wait a minute," Professor Thiesmeyer broke in. "There's a great deal to be learned from exploring the process behind things. Is that what you're saying, Matt?"

"Yes," I said. "I mean this is a liberal arts school, right. We all have to take classes in a bunch of different subjects. I want to be a history teacher and a football coach when all of this is over. Why should I take French? Maybe what the book is saying, and the school, too, by assigning it, is that French class matters even if we never speak a word of French after we graduate. The ends pre-exist in the means."

"I tested out of my language requirement," Long Island laughed again, and the rest of the group laughed with him.

"I'd like to talk to you for a minute after this meeting, Matt," Professor Thiesmeyer said under his breath before shifting gears to the more practical matter of the scheduling process. Later when we were alone he said, "Don't worry about the laughter of your classmates. You're a thinker and you're off to a good start." Then he clapped me on the shoulder and ushered me on my way.

A brisk crinkling of newspaper and the huff of a woman's voice shook me fully awake again. "Pouvez-vous croire ce que cet idiot a dit maintenant? Lisez cette historie! Comment un Americain peut-il soutenir Trump?"

"What did she say about Trump?" Theresa whispered. I didn't know she was awake.

"I think she's reading the newspaper," I said back. "It doesn't sound like she's happy."

"It sounded like she said something about America."

"I think it was, 'How can any American support Trump?' or something like that."

"Oh God," Theresa said. "Is that really what people think? That everyone in America supports him?"

"What are you guys fighting about?" Harper asked, rubbing the sleep out of her eyes.

"We're not fighting, Lulu," I said. "Let's get up and get breakfast."

AFTER our oatmeal, we worked surprisingly fast to pack up our camp. Despite the prospect of nearly five hours of driving, the kids seemed buoyed by the day ahead. Maybe it was the promise of staying in a yurt that night — something we'd never done — or the hope of a day on the waters of Lake Tahoe. Then again, maybe they were finally hitting their stride with the whole life-on-the-road thing.

When everything was packed, Theresa took the kids over to the bathrooms for one last stop before we hit the road. I stood near the back of the Sequoia, re-packing some food for easy access later on.

"Where is your family heading today?" My French neighbor was back.

"We're driving to Lake Tahoe."

"Lake Tahoe? Is there a National Park there?"

The previous night I had explained that our trip was basically a tour of National Parks. "No, no," I said. "This stop is different."

"I have heard of Lake Tahoe. It's a ski resort, yes?"

"It's a big skiing spot, but I hear it's also great in the summer."

"How did you pick it?"

"It's funny, we were at a Fourth of July party back home, and I was telling a friend about our trip. When I told him we'd be in California he said, 'If you love hiking and water sports, you *have* to go to Lake Tahoe.' So I did some research. We'll spend a day there on our way to the Redwoods. How about you guys? What are the plans for today?"

"We're going back into Yosemite. We didn't plan it this way, but there's just so much to see. We want to hike the trail along Yosemite Falls."

"Oh, it looked like you were packing up."

"No, just getting ready," he laughed. "It's always a process. I am used to traveling. I spend so much time in New York. But my wife and son," he tossed a look over his shoulder, "They are still getting used to it here." And something in the way he said *here* made me stop.

"You know," I said, "I probably don't need to say this, but as an American who loves this country, I feel like I have to." His posture stiffened. "I'm so sorry about our president; the things he says, the way he treats other countries and people, the impact he's having on the world. I feel like I have to apologize for my country. I hope you guys know that all the things Trump stands for, that isn't what America is all about."

The Frenchman's face broke into a wide smile, and he laughed his reply. "No, no, my friend, we know this. No one I know thinks of him as America. We know what he is. He comes from here, yes, but he is not America. You do not need to apologize. We know."

"It's just crazy," I said. "We don't know what to do."

"I told you," the Frenchman said, "I spend half of my time in New York. I think of myself as a New Yorker. Trump is *such a New Yorker*. He's an asshole. He says whatever he wants. That's how business is done there. And honestly, I sort of like that about him. In business, I *respect* that. But government is not business. We all see him for what he is. You should hear my wife," he said. "She *hates* him."

"Mine too," I said, pointing to Theresa who was coming down the hill from the bathroom with the kids.

"We are not so different," he laughed and extended his hand to her as she arrived at the Sequoia. And then he said, "Hold on a second," and scurried back into his cabin. He returned a minute later with a slip of paper in his hand and his wife and son trailing sheepishly behind. After we each introduced our families to each other he handed me the paper. On it he'd written his name, phone number, and address in Paris. "So when you come to France you will now have a place to stay. We have plenty of room for friends."

"Plenty of room," his wife added in a heavy accent.

"My turn," I said. Then I pulled out the cardboard box in which I packed away the copies of my novel I'd brought on the trip. "Here's a copy of my book." I signed it, writing my phone number and address in it as well.

"You're an author! A writer! Thank you very much!"

"It's just a story," I said. "I hope to write more."

"Well, maybe we'll make it into the next one," he smiled back. "I hope to see you in Paris soon. Don't forget to vote."

"Au Revoir," I said. As we drove away, for the second time on the trip, I found myself feeling grateful that twenty years ago I had studied French for two semesters.

When I was eight, my great grandfather passed away and we inherited his piano. No one in my family knew how to play the piano at the time, but no matter, my mother insisted we get it. For months after my great-grandfather's passing, there the piano sat, squeezed into our dining room, unused save for as a new napping spot for the cat. All of that changed one spring Sunday.

As my family walked home from church, I noticed my mother carrying one of the purple hymnals that usually sat tucked into the corner of the pew. When I asked her about it, she grew embarrassed and evasive, defensive even, promising that she *asked* to borrow it. "Did you really think I would *steal* a hymnal?"

"Well, no, but why do you want to borrow it?"

"I'm going to teach myself to play the piano," she said. "And then

I'm going to teach you boys how to play. This piano is part of our family. And families honor their roots."

My brother and I flinched. Neither of us particularly *wanted* to play the piano, but we were old enough to know what that particular tone of our mother's voice meant. Soon we'd be playing whether we wanted to or not.

But it turns out we were wrong. With her background in reading music from her days as a high school flute player, my mother *did* successfully end up teaching herself to play the piano, but in the months that followed, despite several harrowing hour-long weekend sessions, she couldn't coax either my brother or me to wrestle our fingers into form. Come summer, it seemed like my mother had given up on the idea that we would ever play together. Relieved, my brother and I went back to our Transformers and Lego sets, content to finally be free of the burden cast by the shadow of the family heirloom in our dining room. But we were foolish to hope that the whole piano-as-part-of-the-family thing was going away; it wasn't.

By Thanksgiving the next year, my mother had grown proficient enough that she could turn to any page in the hymnal and after a few halting practice sessions, flawlessly play the piece. She practiced most nights after dinner, as my father washed the dishes in the kitchen and my brother and I did our best disappearing acts.

One night, however, as I passed her the biscuits, she announced that neither my brother nor I were permitted to go play after dinner. "Tonight," she said, reaching a hand over to pat the piano bench, "You boys are going to help me play."

"But, we don't know how to play," my brother protested.

"I know that," my mother smiled. "That's why you're going to *sing*."

"Sing?" We looked at each other from across the table. "But we don't know how to sing."

"Anybody can sing," my mother shrugged. There was that tone of voice again. And so it was that my brother and I began our schooling in the hymns of the Protestant tradition.

For the next handful of years — from when I was in second grade and my brother was in fifth, until when my brother started high school and had enough homework to beg out of the obligation — my mother would pat her hand on the green piano bench cushion every night after dinner and we would sing — me, always on her right, and my brother always on her left.

To say that I didn't like these sing-alongs wouldn't be fair. I *loathed* them. Loathed them in the way a secretary loathes paper cuts, the way a vegetarian loathes a rare and bloody steak, the way a first-ride-without training-wheels bike rider loathes the bumpy sidewalk near the curve at the end of the block. You get the idea. But my mother was sneaky. She never exactly *forced* us to sing with her. She just gave us "options" that made singing inevitable.

"You don't have to sing if you don't want to. The cat threw up in the basement earlier today. On the rug by the washing machine. I was going to clean it up later, but if you don't feel like singing, you can do it for me now."

It was that kind of thing. Every night. And so, more often than not, we sang.

Her favorite hymn, "Just as I Am," which made its way into every singing session, was particularly painful to my brother and me. Not only was it nearly impossible for our still changing voices to sing well, it also has weird lyrics.

Just as I am, without one plea
But that Thy blood was shed for me
And that Thou bid'st me come to Thee
O Lamb of God, I come! I come
. . .
Just as I am, and waiting not
to rid my soul of one dark blot
to thee whose blood can cleanse each spot
O Lamb of God, I come, I come

ALL that stuff about *blood*. Look, I'm a church going, Bible-reading, pretty thoughtful, adult Christian, and I *still* don't exactly know how I feel about all the talk of cleansing blood that goes on around Jesus. How the hell is a little *kid* supposed to make sense of it?

But looking back now, I have to believe my mother's affinity for "Just As I Am" didn't really have anything to do with the way the hymn sounds (how could it?), nor was it rooted in the blood redemption motif. I think she played that one for us most nights because she was hoping to reassure us, maybe even to reassure herself. The world is very good at telling you you're useless. "Just as I Am," is a promise that no matter how fucked up you are, there is love to be found in this world. I don't need to change for anybody. I am loved. Just As I Am.

Now, as a parent, what I've come to know is that the greatest gifts we give our children seldom take their intended form. When I gave Henry my grandfather's golf clubs, I didn't think he'd used them as swords.

I've never asked her, but I'm sure that by forcing my brother and me to sing the songs of her faith with her each evening, my mother hoped to instill in us a joyful sense of worshipful wonder when contemplating God. Now, I can't speak for my brother, and I wouldn't want to if I could, but that's not what I got out of those long-ago hymn sessions. No, what I got is a near phonically photographic memory of at least the first verse of nearly every damn song in the hymnal.

This repertoire hasn't necessarily brought me any closer to God, but it has saved me a few times. Most notably, when Henry was a toddler and regularly insisted that I not only hold him, but also look him in the eye while he tried to cram his "Fresha" (Some kids call it a "binky," Henry called it a "Fresha") into my mouth as I sang during church. No worries, Henry. I don't need to look at the words. I know this one by heart.

But every once in a while, when I'm not thinking along these lines at all, one of those long-ago hymns will pop into my head full volume, and refuse to leave until I at least acknowledge its existence. I guess in this way the hymns of my youth sort of serve as a soundtrack for my soul.

But don't tell my mother. The last thing I want is for her to think those post-dinner torture sessions did me some good. Even if that's the truth.

Is there anything as complicated as a child's relationship with his parents?

Henry — on the shore of Tioga Lake. Inyo National Forest. Mono County, California.

As we made our way through the winding roads of Yosemite toward Lake Tahoe, I rolled down the windows of the Sequoia and blasted a thumb-selected soundtrack of my favorite artists ranging from the Avett Brothers to Counting Crows to The Red Hot Chili Peppers. This is something I love to do and something my kids truly hate. To me there are few things on earth better than listening to some of the best music ever made while viewing some of the most majestic vistas on planet earth, but the joy of such an experience is greatly diminished by the persistent chorus of complaints, otherwise known as bitching from the backseat, that inevitably ensues whenever I try to escape into my music for a while.

I can usually ignore them for a song or two, but eventually either Theresa or I will have to get mad at the kids, tell them to suck it up (or something like that), before turning up the next song up even louder (that'll show 'em). This approach generally works for a while, but inevitably I end up looking in the rearview mirror and seeing the looks on my kids' faces. Looks that seem a whole lot like what I imagine *my* face must have looked like when my mother used to make me sit on that piano bench next to her after dinner. Such a battle was in full froth when we decided to cut the music and pull over for lunch at a picnic area overlooking Tioga Lake in the Mammoth Lakes region of Northern Yosemite.

Northern Yosemite is like an underrated Bob Dylan song. By default, everybody knows it's good, maybe even borderline-great — this is Dylan we're talking about here — but it's never going to get its proper due because of the popularity and notoriety of what it's always compared to. Think "In Search of Little Sadie" and "Belle Isle" from *Self Portrait* against "Like a Rolling Stone" and "Tangled Up in Blue" from *Highway 61* and *Blood on the Tracks*, respectively. Good as the former are, they'll never get as much airtime as the latter. The same is true when it comes to the sights of Northern Yosemite compared to the likes of El Capitan, Tunnel View and Glacier Point. But, Northern Yosemite left me speechless in ways that the crowded icons to the south couldn't touch.

After lunch we clambered down the steep roadside slope that leads to the lapping shore of Tioga Lake. I have lived in the city across an unkempt street from the housing projects on a block the mayor forgot. And also in a tidy apartment tucked in the shadow of green New England mountains on a well-manicured campus where every building carried a name. Early in our marriage, Theresa and I wrestled with a small place in a lakeside village in upstate New York, trying our best to make it our own. And when we started our family, we found a house to call our home.

But sitting in the stillness with my wife and three children on the shore of a mountain lake stirred in me a sense of belonging I've never known before. The water somehow both opaquely blue and clear. A beard of thick pine forest growing out of the grassy meadow. Snowcapped mountains whose edges kissed the sky. A silence true and swallowing. The air, fresh and light. I could see myself there forever.

When we got back into the Sequoia, I reached for my phone to cue up the next song on the soundtrack.

"Dad, wait." Henry said. "How about we do that thing where each of us picks a song?"

"Henry, the last time we did that, you played three songs in a row that either were full of curse words, made sexual references that aren't appropriate for family car rides, or whose lyrics were all about bragging about how much money the dude was making. You're censored."

"Come on, Dad. I'll pick a better one this time, I promise."

"Okay, but this is your last chance. We'll go in reverse age order. Harper you're up first."

Harper picked Lady Gaga's, "Million Reasons," as usual, and Theresa and I sang along. Max dialed up, "High Hopes," by Panic at the Disco and I dance-drove to the beat, acting like a goofball to try to get Max to laugh. Then I passed the phone to Henry and held my breath. "I found this one the other day," he said. "Can we roll down the windows? Let's turn it up. It's acapella."

> *Oh Lord, my God*
> *When I, in awesome wonder*
> *Consider all the worlds Thy hands have made*
> *I see the stars, I hear the rolling thunder*

Thy power throughout the universe displayed
Then sings my soul, my Savior God to Thee
How great Thou art, how great Thou art
Then sings my soul, my Savior God to Thee
How great Thou art, how great Thou art.

As the words and the wind washed over us, I drove on, both stunned and grateful. Stunned that my son could find his way to a song I used to sing with my mother after dinner. And grateful for words that spoke so clearly to the stirrings of my heart. How Great Thou Art, indeed.

EVEN though it's just off a fairly busy road, the William Kent Campground in Lake Tahoe has a rustic feel (no showers or laundry facilities on site. No electricity or toilet paper in the bathrooms. Lots of bear-proofing required). We unpacked our things from the car and settled into the yurt, which, by nature of its canvas roof and bunk beds, felt huge and luxurious after two nights of sleeping in the dirt. Then we drove into Tahoe City in search of a good place to eat and a grocery store where we could restock our food supply.

When we got back to the yurt, we packed and locked the bear box and then headed across the road to wash off in the lake. The sun set as we were swimming, turning the lake into a pool of orange, yellow and red that mirrored the swirls of the sky.

I floated out past my shoulders and lay on my back looking up at the growing night. And I felt happy again. Happy and home. Just as I am.

Here and There
(Day 14. *Lake Tahoe*)

WE ARRIVED AT SAND Harbor on the Nevada shore of Lake Tahoe just after 8:00 a.m.. It was already growing crowded, so I hustled toward the beach with our camp chairs and a cooler full of food, while Theresa slapped sunscreen on the kids in the parking lot. Other families plopped their things down close to the main building where the bathrooms and lifeguard stands are located, but I hunted along the further shore, looking for a less crowded spot.

Eventually I found a half-buried, table-sized boulder nestled in a stretch of smooth sand, and spread out our towels next to it in the glow of the still rising sun. Within twenty minutes the narrow beach around us was packed with people, but with the boulder behind us, and the curve of the shore flanking us to our right, we had plenty of room to sprawl without fear of stepping on strangers.

Theresa and I sat together watching the kids dig a deep hole in the sand near the tideline: a pool for dipping their feet in, they told us. Henry took charge. He pulled off his Crocs and gave one to Max instructing him to use it to help him burrow while Harper was tasked with dog-digging the wet sand into the rough outlines of a wall. For half an hour, our children wrestled with the water — making momentary progress only to have Tahoe's tide repeatedly wash over their work.

But they didn't give up. Each time the water made a sloppy mess of what they'd built, they sprang back into action. Shouting out gleeful orders to each other and re-digging whatever was washed away. In a final effort, Henry laid himself in front of their sloshy sand dam, hoping to use his body to shield it from the water long enough for them to establish a structure that would last.

"That's pretty noble of you, Henry. Giving yourself up for the cause. You might get sand in your shorts though."

"I don't care," he said. "If I lay here long enough, we'll be able to build something the waters won't reach." But even as he said this, a wave crashed over his back and erased their progress. Still undeterred, Max and Harper scurried frantically to slosh the water away from the wall and build it back up again, but this time Henry did not carry on. He stood up. "What's the point of this anyway? It all just gets wiped out in the end."

"That's true," I responded. "The water always wins."

"I guess this is pretty stupid then. I mean it's kind of useless."

"It's not useless," I said. "It's fun, right?"

"Yeah, it's fun, but nothing we do lasts more than a minute. What's the point?"

"The fun is the point," I said. And I suddenly realized I wasn't just saying some throwaway line.

*Henry, Max and Harper — holding back the tide. Sand Harbor.
Lake Tahoe Nevada State Park.*

EVERY summer when I was a kid, my family spent the first two weeks of August on Cape Cod. As much as that makes me sound like a country club kid, that wasn't the case at all — for most of those years, my mom stayed at home and my dad worked for The American Red Cross. There wasn't a ton of money kickin' around for cool shoes and stonewashed jeans. Still, my parents honeymooned on the Cape and were committed to going back each year, even if it meant saving every spare penny to afford the trip. Which is exactly what they did.

We usually stayed in modest places. The one I remember best was a one-bedroom efficiency apartment attached to a bed and breakfast. My parents arranged with the inn owners for the double bed to be dragged from the bedroom to the living room, a single bed to be set up in its place and a rollaway cot to be tucked into the corner behind the bathroom door. My brother and I slept in what was once the apartment's bedroom while my parents set up shop in the old living room in plain sight of the stove. We showered outside in a rigged up closet, and did our laundry once a week at the sweaty Laundromat across from the grocery store. To a kid it was cozy and nice — more than enough space. Looking back though I see my parents were making due as best as they could.

During those trips we mostly spent our days at the beach. Taking long walks out to rocky piers, flying kites, swimming in the Nantucket Sound, and building intricate castles in the sand. Once a summer, my father would spend the better part of a morning building a sand sculpture: a seashell-strewn lobster, a sprawling starfish, or a clomping crab. His process was always the same. He would trace the shape out in the sand, dig a deep moat around the outer edges and pile the excess sand high inside the lines, then he'd pat the sand firm, a process augmented by frequent buckets of ocean water splashed on the structure by my brother and me. Once that was over, he'd dig in with the edge of a plastic shovel until some over-sized sea creature emerged from what once was an innocuous plot of beach.

Once he was finished with the sculpture, my dad would settle in next to my mom with his feet in the sand and spend the rest of the day watching as everyone from shirtless dudes in baggy surfer shorts to frumpy old ladies in swimming caps paused on their way down the beach to admire his work. By late afternoon, the August sun inevitably faded the sculpture's firmness, but the outline was always still there. Even as we packed up our things and headed back up the cottage-lined street for dinner.

Most evenings, we returned to the water's edge. Sometimes we'd bring along an old football to toss back and forth. Sometimes we would look for shells and storm-tossed treasures amidst the seaweed and the tide. And sometimes we'd just sit and watch as the sunset painted the sky, and the sandpipers raced the waves in search of their evening meal. But the one thing that was always constant, the one thing that never changed, was by the time we returned to the water, my father's sand sculpture was gone. Erased by the careless strides of the early evening beachcombers or the swell of the rising tide. No matter how magnificent in the morning, nothing ever remained.

Nothing human is eternal. Our work. Our relationships. All of the "have-to" tasks that fill our days. Our lives are waves on the shore of the universe. Colors in a sky growing dark. Sand shaped beautifully for a moment until the feet of time trample it flat.

But I can still smell the water from those salty summer days. Hear my bucket crunch against the sand. See the sun splash across my father's back, as his shadow falls long up the beach to where my mother lay on her belly, watching him dig in the sand.

There, a sunburnt kid squints out toward his future — a sandy red bucket clutched tight in his hand. Here, a forty-something father stands on the shore of a California lake watching his children play at his feet. The moment is the same.

If you told me, back when I was a kid on the Cape, that things would go on like that forever, I would have believed every single word. But now I know better. Now I understand. Forever is different. It's both Here *and* There.

AFTER yet another lunch of peanut butter smeared bagels with sliced bananas on top, Theresa pulled her hat over her eyes and drifted into an open-mouthed nap. At Harper's request, the kids and I marched off toward a cluster of boulders that rose out of the water in a line.

Lake Tahoe's boulders are the stuff of postcard legend, and we were not alone in scrambling up them to test our mettle by jumping off into the blue chop below. There were square-pecked bros sprinting off edges into full-speed flips, and teenage girls daring their bikini tops to stay on as they twisted toward the water. But there was also a pack of kids around Henry's age who followed our progress as we climbed and jumped off of each rock along the shore. For about an hour, we became a sort of tribe.

In the way of kids, we never introduced ourselves or asked where they were from. Instead we helped each other find the easiest path up the rocks. And once we all safely made it to the top, the bravest of us would test out the jump, hoping to help the others avoid breaking a bone on an unseen shallow ledge below. Once in the water, the first jumper would shout out instructions up to the rest of us.

It quickly became an unspoken truth that Harper would neither be the first nor last person in the tribe to jump. Also, if an initially reasonable looking jump proved to be too difficult for her: the distance to be cleared too wide, the landing pool too specific, then the group would be waved down off the rock and we'd collectively swim to our next adventure.

Seriously, this happened more than once.

Finally, the other kids were called away by a woman whom I assume was one of their mothers. With nothing more than a brisk set of nods, they walked out of our lives as quickly as they walked in.

My muscles ached and there was a sweet, deep exhaustion settling into my bones that warned against trying to swim out to the farthest rock from shore, when Max, slightly out of breath and nodding his head toward the open water asked, "Ready, Dad?".

"No, Max. Those rocks are too far away from the shore. If we get into trouble no lifeguard will be able to save us."

Henry scoffed, "We won't need saving, Dad. Come on." As he slapped my arm reassuringly, I felt the flab where my triceps muscles used to be flop in the wind. Harper was already climbing down toward the water.

I see the scene unfold from above. The boys in the lead, making small wakes as their arms splash out in front of them. Carving a path toward the next adventure. Me, gasping and awkward, making my way as best I can with Harper's arms tight around my neck. Her body floating loosely between my frog-kicking legs.

About half way there, my breath short and my muscles burning, I thought of turning back. The bottom of the lake seemed fathoms below; I was sure I couldn't make it. But the boys were well out in front of me now. I couldn't leave them. I had to go on.

Harper sounded worried, "Are you okay, Daddy?"

"Just kick for me a bit, sweetheart. Daddy needs some help."

Once we were all on top of the boulder, we decided it was too dangerous to jump. So we just sat there alone and quiet for a while, surrounded by water on all sides, gathering our strength for the swim back to shore.

WEST Shore Sports is one of those stores you often find in resort towns. We rented three kayaks — two, two-person and one, one-person —and arranged to meet the guy at the launch point across from our yurt.

It took us ten minutes of full-froth arguing on the beach before we settled on the kayak pairings. This is something I still haven't figured out about parenting. Sometimes it seems like my kids want nothing to do with me. They roll their eyes when I engage strangers in conversation, walk ten steps ahead of me when we're out in public, say they hate my music, and generally ignore any advice I give them about homework and sports. But then other times they fight — almost to the point of tears — over who will get to ride next to me on the sidewalk during a bike ride around town, or, in this case, who will get to sit at the bow of my kayak as we paddle along the shore of the lake.

When we finally pushed off, Theresa took the lead in the single, the boys steered the second together, splashing and complaining of their respective incompetence all the way, and Harper and I brought up the rear, me doing most of the paddling while Harper shouted out orders and observations over her shoulder.

"Isn't this beautiful, Matt?" Theresa beamed. "I mean, just look at it. It's perfect." *Perfect?* Shit, I hadn't noticed. Here she was feeling all Zen and peaceful and I was busy trying to figure out a way to resist the urge to go and capsize my boys' kayak and leave them for dead. Some days I find my kids' general nonsense hilarious and other days it makes me want to put my head through a wall.

But I swallowed hard, "Yeah. It's amazing. Totally unreal." She didn't need to deal with that crap. I mean when's the next time she'll be on Lake Tahoe? Probably never again, right? I wanted her to enjoy it. One of us ought to.

THE guy from the shop was waiting for us on the shore when we pulled up. We were the last renters of the day, and I got the feeling that he wanted to get the boats out of the water and onto their racks as quickly as possible, but we needed to sign some paperwork back in the shop before we took off.

These kayaks were not light, especially the two-person ones, so

I grabbed the other end as the shop guy dragged it up the beach and together we carried it across the parking lot to the side of the boathouse where he'd lock them up for the night. There was part of me that was doing this to be nice and part of me that was doing it to get a little space from the boys who were still gripping with each other about who was to blame for the less-than-straight-path they took on their way back to shore. Space is space. I'll take what I can get. Even if it means carrying an awkward kayak with a stranger.

"You guys have fun out there?" he asked.

"It's beautiful," I replied without answering his question. "You get out on the water much?"

"Not really. I've lived here all my life. I'm kind of used to it."

"Lived here all your life, huh. You probably get sick of all the tourists." We were at the boathouse now and on the count of three we lifted the kayak upside down and on to the highest shelf on the rack.

"No. It's just how it is."

"Yeah. That's funny," I said. "I guess after a while almost any-thing can feel normal." But what I was really thinking is, how sad. Here this guy is, living in this amazing place, and he can't really appreciate it. He doesn't seem to see how lucky he is.

As we turned to walk back toward the beach I heard Max's strained voice. "They went around the corner, Henry." And when the kayak guy and I rounded the corner of the building, we saw my boys coming toward us, struggling to carry the other two-per-son kayak up to the rack.

"What are you guys doing?" I asked. "You can just go chill with mom. We got this."

"We figured we would help, Dad," Henry replied. "It's no prob-lem."

When we got back to the shop, I went in to sign the return papers and pick up our receipt while Theresa waited in the Sequoia with the kids.

"I'm waiving the docking fee," the shop guy said. "You guys are, like, the only customers ever to help me drag the boats up to the rack. Pretty wild," he laughed. "You're doing something right with those boys, sir. No kidding."

I nodded and grabbed the papers. "Yeah, they surprise me sometimes," I said.

By the time we got back to the yurt everyone was hungry and tired. We were low on food and no one had the energy to be creative with whatever was left in the cooler. I noticed a general store down the road a piece, so we decided to grab our towels and head over. We'd pick up whatever we could find there, then eat our "meal" picnic style in the park where we swam the previous night, before washing off again in the lake and getting back to bed.

My parents used to tell this story of how, when my brother was little, he refused to eat dinner unless his plate was surrounded by his collection of plastic toy horses. I went through a stage where I wouldn't eat hot dogs unless my mother cut the skin off of them first. As my kids wandered the aisles, picking up food to eat: a granola bar, an apple, a bag of baby carrots, a just-ripe avocado, this weird sense of pride swelled in my heart. Here were my kids, wandering the aisles of a general store in California, not only picking out food to eat, but doing their best to make sure they were eating a balanced meal.

We ate our dinner in the shade of a tree looking out at the lake. When we were done we went down to the water and jumped in for the last dip of the day. When we climbed out there was another couple on the beach. An older guy with a long beard and a much younger looking woman who, nevertheless, seemed to be his traveling partner. I noticed two motorcycles parked next to each other in the lot. I struck up a conversation with them as I was toweling off.

"You guys been riding very long?"

When the girl spoke, the lift in her voice made her seem like a teenager. "We just came from the Redwoods. We've been riding all day."

"The Redwoods, huh? That's where we're heading next. We're out here from Buffalo. We've been circling around for two weeks now." Then I told them where we'd been and where we were going.

The man smiled back at me through his beard. "That's the same trip we're taking, basically. Only in reverse."

"So weird," the girl laughed. "It's like that circle has an energy, right? Gotta see the flow."

I nodded. "How were the Redwoods?"

"Man, like nothing you've ever seen." The guy's eyes glowed. "I've been there before when I was a kid, but I wanted her to see it. We wanted to see it together is what I mean." The girl twisted her arms around his waist in reply and he laughed while looking down at her.

I felt a tug on my shorts and turned around to see Max. Henry was standing with him and Theresa and Harper were making their way toward us up the beach. When everyone was together I introduced them to the riders. We made small talk for a while, and then we said our goodbyes and made our way back across the street toward the yurt.

In the growing twilight, I built a fire and bear-proofed the campsite for the night while Theresa ushered the kids back and forth from the bathroom — brushing their teeth, getting their PJs on. Then we sat together in silence around the fire as the moon rose into the still blue sky.

Maybe that's the trick in this whole Act of Becoming thing. Maybe the path isn't supposed to lead you to perfect. Maybe perfect is the *problem*. Maybe if you really want to have anything worth holding onto, you've got to first figure out how to let a whole bunch of other stuff go.

I'm never going to be a perfect dad, an always-adequate husband, or even a mostly-sensible man, but at least I can say I gave my loved ones this. A moonrise around the campfire and the lakeside silence of a California night.

Waiting for the Bear

*(Days 15 and 16. Lake Tahoe — Redding, California —
Patrick's Point & Redwoods)*

THE NIGHT BEFORE, AS we gathered our supplies for dinner at the general store, the guy who bagged the groceries told me a story of how earlier that afternoon he'd gone into his backyard to refill the birdfeeders only to find a mother black bear and her two cubs rooting around in the seeds and suet. He held up his phone as proof.

"I've always wanted to see a bear in the wild," I told him.

"Here's a good place for that," he said plainly. "We've got bears all over. But like I said, it's best to just let them be when you find them."

"Oh, I just want to see one, that's all. I'm not hoping for anything more than that." Theresa rolled her eyes and Harper tugged at my shirt. Both of them knew of my desire to see a bear and mutually disapproved of it heartily. The boys on the other hand played along with me every time I talked about it, but I also noticed they seemed to pick up their voices wherever we were off hiking in the woods together. Maybe *they* were just bluffing about wanting to see a bear, but I wasn't.

RIGHT before I went to college, my mother bought me a book of daily devotionals. The book followed the lectionary schedule, directing readers to first explore a biblical passage then read a one page reflection, written by a new author from a different denominational background each week, and wrapped things up with a prayer or "thought for the day" which was meant to be a mantra to carry with you on your way. Sometimes these reflections were straight-up biblical analysis, and sometimes they were only tangentially connected to The Word. Most times though the authors sought to connect the contemporary world to some element of the text.

My guess is my mom gave me this gift because she hoped I wouldn't walk away from my faith as I walked onto my college campus. No worries there. Though I wasn't in the campus choir or anything like that, I regularly attended local churches throughout my college career, doing my best to never visit the same one two weeks in a row. I even found my way to mosques, temples, and shrines, as I sought to authenticate and test my beliefs against the ways of the world. I'm not sure me bowing to Mecca with a bunch of old Muslim dudes was what my mother had in mind when she gave me the devotional, but in a weird way, the practice of starting each day by reflecting on something larger than myself inspired me to push my faith beyond the sometimes easy answers and contrite phrases of Sunday Services.

Over the years, this practice of starting my day by reading the Bible and an associated reflection evolved into a sort-of mini meditation session. Each day over breakfast I'd set some time aside. Sometimes I'd journal, sometimes I'd just sit in silence holding my coffee and trying to get my head around the day, and sometimes I'd thumb back through the previous pages, re-reading favorite sections and committing particular passages to heart.

Then Theresa and I got married, secured jobs, bought a house and started having kids. Life became "full" and "busy." I've always thought of myself as a morning person, but as my days became more packed with activities it became harder and harder to wake up before the sun to exercise and read. The things I once treasured about the beginning of my day began to feel like burdensome "have tos." I still tried to keep up with my routine, but I wasn't always happy about it; often just going through the motions, or beating myself up whenever I missed a day or two.

What's weird is I didn't set out to live this way. It's the inertia of life. If you're not always paying attention, riding the brakes and pulling the ripcord of "No," then before long you're in this whirlwind where everything just feels like a trap.

Theresa came home from work one late December night to find me muttering to myself in the basement as I tried to organize the kids' Christmas gifts into wrapping piles; a method I hoped would help us compartmentalize the work. I barely acknowledged her when she said hello and before long we were having one of our increasingly common "discussions" about the busy nature of our life together. Like most such arguments this one was broad and sprawling — fueled by exhaustion and the stress of trying to meet the increasing demands of our middle-class lifestyle. When I said something about not even having enough time to read the Bible anymore, Theresa shot back, "Be the person you want to be, Matt!" then stormed up the stairs and switched off the light. Something about that directive struck a chord with me, so before I closed my eyes that night, I set my alarm early with plans to start anew.

The next morning, as I sat looking at my coffee steam, my Bible open to the designated passage waiting to be read, I decided to ignore its invitation and instead write down a list of just exactly who I wanted to be. Here's what it said:

BE THE PERSON YOU WANT TO BE
- Run every day / stay physically fit and active.
- Wake-up early and don't be tired - stay up late.
- Read books of my choice (1 a month).
- Play the guitar / harmonica.
- Write every day.
- Be a good husband — caring, thoughtful, sensitive, and supportive.
- Be a good, hands-on father — play with my kids, be consistent with my discipline, be a good role model (happy, healthy, and loving).
- Make meaningful connections with the students I teach.
- Spend time outside every day.
- Be politically aware (read the newspaper).
- Attend church / seek spirituality
- Maintain / cultivate meaningful friendships.
- Be a leader at school
- Be happy, funny, creative, intense, kind, reasonable, thoughtful, sensitive, sincere, and strong (mentally, physically and spiritually).
- Relaxed, yet earnest.
- Flexible — physically and mentally.
- Comfortable — jeans and twill vs. khakis and oxfords.
- Drink beer.
- Follow sports.
- Be consistent and reliable (don't back out of things or over-commit myself).

Taken as a whole these are noble goals, but they also feel impossible. Like how can you stay up late *and* get up early? And what does drinking beer have to do with anything? But just because my list is full of contradictions and shrugs away the reality of the number of hours in a day, doesn't mean it isn't real. That list *is* who I want to be. But here's a harsh reality of adult life: it's damn near impossible to "Be the person you want to be" all the time. Sometimes you have to settle. Sometimes you've got to let go. Instead of always striving to be your mythical "best self," sometimes you've got to just accept the person you are.

But here's the thing, even as I write this, sure of its objective truth, the words: *settle, accept,* and *letting go* also make me want to vomit. I mean, how *soft*, right? What's the difference between acceptance and giving up? Where do you draw the line?

WHEN I awoke before the others to find it was cold enough outside of my sleeping bag to need a fire, the thought of rolling back over to grab a few more winks was compelling, but so too was the quiet of the Lake Tahoe morning. So I got dressed and closed the door of the yurt behind me. Then, after stirring last night's ashes underneath some newly gathered branches, I sat down at the campsite's picnic table with a cup of coffee and a small pile of books spread out before me hoping to find inspiration in either The Word or the World.

"What are you doing out here, Dad?" Henry stood before me, wrapped in a hoodie and sweatpants, hugging himself toward warmth and shifting back and forth on his feet. I hadn't heard him open the yurt's door.

"Reading," I smiled back at him. "And waiting for the bear."

"Wait, you saw a bear! For real?"

"No," I said. "That's what I'm waiting for."

"Dad. *Why?*"

"Because I think it would be cool. That's all," I shrugged. "A bear is the ultimate spirit of the woods. Plus, I figure, if an Elk can walk up next to me when I'm sitting outside of our tent in the Grand Canyon, a bear just might amble by while I'm out here. This is *bear country* after all." Then I patted the bench next to me. "Sit down." Henry stood by the fire for another moment before slouching down next to me and resting his head on my shoulder.

"Is that a list?"

"Yeah," I said as I tucked *Be The Person You Want To Be* back into my Bible. "That's a story for another day."

"What are you reading?"

"The Bible and this." I held up the *Tao Te Ching*.

"That's a little book. What is it?"

"This is the *Tao Te Ching*, which means, *The Book of the Way*."

"Why do you have it?"

"I read it sometimes. It's important to me. Its chapters are like little poems. Can I read you one of my favorites?"

"Sure," he said, so I turned to a dog-eared page.

> *Nothing in the world*
> *Is as soft and yielding as water.*
> *Yet for dissolving the hard and inflexible,*
> *Nothing can surpass it.*
>
> *The soft overcomes the hard;*
> *The gentle overcomes the rigid.*
> *Everyone knows this is true,*
> *But few can put it into practice.*
>
> *Therefore the Master remains*
> *Serene in the midst of sorrow.*
> *Evil cannot enter his heart.*
> *Because he has given up helping,*
> *He is people's greatest help.*
>
> *True words seem paradoxical.*

"Pretty cool to think about, right?" I nudged Henry with my elbow.

"What?"

"That water is both totally passive and supremely powerful. Maybe the same is true for us."

"Yeah. Maybe." He sat up straight and threw the twig he'd been breaking up into little pieces into the fire. "Can I have breakfast now?"

"Sure."

ONCE the others were up and fed, we packed the car and walked over to the lake for one more look. Four hours of driving awaited us; we wanted to stretch our legs before we got on the road. We were heading toward a stopover stay at an Airbnb I found in Redding, California. Nothing special to look forward to. Just a necessary break in the trip; a chance to take a shower, sleep in a bed and cook a meal on a proper stove.

By the time we reached Redding, it was late afternoon and the mercury hung around one hundred degrees. Our rented place was in a paved planned community whose streets all looked the same — something the online description failed to mention. Also left out was the fact that our "charming" place was one side of a duplex. It's not that I'm opposed to sharing a wall with somebody; I lived in apartments for years. But as we pulled up the driveway, something about the shady-looking dude wearing a ratty tank top and leaning back on two legs of his chair, smoking a cigarette in front of our door gave me pause.

"Is this the place?" Theresa asked.

"Yeah. Looks like it. Everybody grab a bag and we'll head inside." By the time all of us were out of the Sequoia, our neighbor had disappeared.

Theresa and I unloaded the car while the kids rushed into the living room to watch TV in the glory of the air-conditioning. We sat together in the kitchen drawing up a quick grocery list and marveling at the creature comforts of the place. Theresa wanted to get started on the laundry so I agreed to head to the store.

When I opened the door again, I was hit by a palpable wave of heat. Then I smelled smoke. Our neighbor was back at his spot.

"Man, it's hot," I said as I locked my wife and children inside behind me.

"This is nothing. At least it's not wet like where I'm from."

"Oh yeah, where are you from?" I asked, resisting the temptation to ask the other questions on my mind: *Why are you smoking outside of our apartment? Are you running a meth ring out of your garage? Will my family still be alive when I return with the groceries?* He tapped his shirt in reply and drew in a long drag on his cigarette.

"Alabama?" I asked. He nodded. His T-shirt bragged of the Crimson Tide's most recent National Championship. "Man, you're almost as far away from home as we are."

"That right? Where you from?

"The Buffalo area."

"Cold up there. That's what they say."

"In the winter it's cold for sure. Lots of snow too. But summers are nice."

"How come y'all out here then?"

"Just taking in the sights. Doing a loop through the national parks and whatnot." He nodded and took another drag. If I'm being honest, I started talking to him because I wanted to give my creep radar, which was buzzing like crazy when we first pulled in, a chance to settle down. I wanted to see if the guy seemed okay. If he could carry on a conversation. So far, the reviews were mixed.

"What brought you out here from Alabama?" I asked.

"My mom moved out here. Then my brother and I followed her. They both moved back now though. It's just me out here now."

"What do you do for work?" I asked. I didn't care if it was a nosy question. It was after three o'clock on a Wednesday in August and the guy was just chilling out at home. I was about to head to the store and leave my family behind. Before I left, I *needed* to know if this guy was a serial killer just waiting around in between gigs or not. Anyway, asking him if he was gainfully employed seemed fair enough.

"Nothing," he said.

"Nice gig." I laughed.

"How about you?" he said. "What do y'all do for work?"

"I'm a teacher." I said.

"Teacher, huh? That's funny." He stood up and tossed his cigarette butt into the stones in front of the stoop. "I came out here for school."

"Oh, no way. Are you going to be a teacher?"

"Not likely," he said. "I'm not in school anymore." He took his hat off and wiped his brow with the back of his wrist. For the first time I got a good look at his face. He was maybe twenty. He tossed his hat in the chair and let out a long sigh.

"Well there are a lot of ways to be happy. That's what I tell my students, anyway. School isn't for everyone."

"No, it's not," he said flatly. "In fact, seems like that's the way they make it." His hand was on his doorknob now. "You folks staying long?"

"No. We'll be gone tomorrow."

"Maybe I won't see you then." He turned toward me and we shook hands in the heat.

"Well, good luck either way," I said. He nodded and walked into his apartment without saying another word. I must have walked over twenty cigarette butts on my way to the car.

ONE time, when Henry and Max were really little and my dad was really sick, I almost blacked out while teaching *The Adventures of Huckleberry Finn* because I was so stressed out and sleep deprived. And another time, for like three hours one Saturday morning, I couldn't stop sweating. It was just pouring off me and all I did was wake up and drink coffee. But I've seen a few people have panic attacks, and the way they looked was sort of how I felt standing in the foyer of the grocery store in Redding.

Corporate pop. Fluorescent lighting. Piped-in jazz. Pimply-faced teens in awkward-fitting uniforms slicing cold-cut meat into plastic bags. And aisle after aisle of bright boxes of processed food. Plastic bottles of pop. Jugs of milk. Boxes of laundry detergent packaged in pods which teenagers sometimes eat for fun. And a woman somewhere between my age and the age of my mother, looking all sad and broken down, who asked me in a heavy latina accent, "Did you find everything you need?"

Maybe it was the heat finally getting to me. Maybe my southern friend was smoking something other than tobacco and I got a secondhand hit. Then again, maybe, by that point in the trip, I had been "away from it all" long enough to notice that what passes for every-day-normal is really something *quite* different. Whatever was going on, I felt like I couldn't breathe in that store. I paid as quickly as I could then scooped up my bags and hustled out into the blazing heat. The thermometer in the Sequoia read 107.

When I returned to our rental, the neighbor was nowhere in sight. The kids were glued to the TV, and Theresa was taking a shower. I unloaded the groceries and cooked up a batch of "Super Nachos" for dinner, an invention I created on one of those nights when the kids were all little and Theresa was off at work. We sat around the dining room table and ate our food with real silverware and a roof over our heads. We had ice cream out of a box for dessert.

I don't know anything about that kid who was our neighbor in Redding. I assumed a lot about him and for that I feel ashamed. I don't know anything about the woman who rented us her place for the night either — other than what I surmised from the Biblical passages she had framed all over her walls. I guess in the end, people are mostly unknowable. Places too. We usually see what we expect.

MAX and I were the first ones up the next morning, so we put together a full breakfast of bacon and eggs for everybody. I let him take the lead, and when everything was all set, we woke up the others.

We took the relatively short drive from Redding to Patrick's Point, a small coastal state park in Trinidad, California, just twenty minutes south of Redwoods National Park. Even though there are no Redwoods in Patrick's Point, we chose to stay there anyway because of its proximity to both the ocean and the trees. Turns out there were other attractions to see there as well.

"Take note of the sign, please," the park ranger said as she handed me a camp map. I glanced at the poster hanging on the side of the station on which appeared a snarling mountain lion and an abundance of red ink.

"You've had some lions in the area?" I asked without finishing reading the poster.

The ranger looked at me from underneath the visor of her wide-brimmed hat. "That's right. Lions and bears."

"What, no tigers?" I joked. She didn't smile. "You know, like the song from the Wizard of Oz? *'Lions and Tigers and Bears. Oh My!'*"

"It's been a dangerous summer, sir."

I leaned my head out the window, crooked my elbow on the side of the car door and slid closer to her while whispering out of the side of my mouth. "We've been traveling out this way for a couple of weeks now. We've seen a lot of these signs. I've read up on what to do and all, and I appreciate the warning. You can be certain we'll be careful. It's just we're trying not to freak out the kids too much."

The ranger put her hands on her knees and leaned forward, her face just inches away from mine. I slid my head back into the car as she spoke to all of us. "This is a serious situation. Mom and Dad, I wouldn't let the kids out of my sight if I were you. And if you go walking around camp, I'd carry a knife or a large stick with you at all times." She stood up and patted the top of the car. "You folks enjoy your stay."

Enjoy your stay? S-u-u-re we will. Nothing to worry about here. Just so long as we don't get mauled or eaten. "Thank you *very* much, ranger," I said before pulling away. "Appreciate the warning."

"Geez, Matt" Theresa's face was etched with fear. "That's horrible."

"I'm sure we'll be fine." I turned back to face my children. "Kids, you heard what the ranger said. Just stick to the trails. Our campsite isn't too far from the showers. We should be fine. No worries."

"That's not what the ranger said," Henry retorted.

"Yeah, she said we should carry a stick and a knife, Dad."

"She just wants us to be careful, Harper."

"Why didn't she say that then?" asked Max.

"She did. I mean, that's kind of what she said."

"She said a stick and a *knife*." Harper was growing desperate.

"We'll be fine, sweetheart. Besides, I kind of *want* to see a bear."

"We know *you* do, Dad." She rolled her eyes and turned toward the window. "Who wants to carry a *knife*?"

Rilke once wrote, "Let everything happen to you. Beauty and Terror. Just keep going. No feeling is final." I love that quote.

I'm all for being prepared and for keeping things safe. No need to take *stupid* risks. But there's a line there too, you know? You can't bubble-wrap your kids. Sometimes if you want to experience beauty with a capital B you've got to stomach a little Terror along the way.

What the hell was that ranger thinking?

WE found our campsite carved into a dense grove of spruce trees. Thanks to the ranger's warning, the kids hung close as Theresa and I set up the tent and figured out how to bear-proof the place for the night. Soon Max discovered that if you stood on the picnic table the sky opened up between the trunks of the trees and you could see the churning Pacific in the distance. The pounding tide provided the soundtrack for our unpacking. After we got settled, we found there was enough time to do some exploring before dinner, so we climbed back into the Sequoia and headed to the Redwoods Visitor Center in Orick.

Redwoods National Park has a totally different feel from the other parks we visited. The government still has its fingerprints on it and all, but they don't smear the glass in quite the same way as they do in the other parks. It's like they kind of want you to figure it out for yourself. I don't mean like when you're looking for a particular kind of bathroom fixture in Home Depot and spend twenty minutes walking around the dingy isles looking for a guy in an orange apron to help you. It's not frustrating like that. What I mean is you don't feel pulled along by some imaginary string.

THE first thing that surprised me about coastal Redwoods is they don't look as red as Sequoia trees. And while both species are enormous, Redwoods are noticeably taller; Sequoias are squat and girthy by comparison. I suppose a person might say, "Big trees are big trees," to which I'd retort, that's easy to say until you stand in the shadow of a Redwood. Looking up from the ground to the upper branches of one of these trees made me feel like a grain of sand at the bottom of the ocean.

We headed toward a trail I'd read about that circles past Trillium Falls. Max and Henry raced up the ferny switchbacks as the trail climbed over 400 feet into the deeper woods, while Harper hung back with Theresa and me, her neck set at a stark angle to search for sunlight in the upper branches. An umbrella of blended shades and shadows sheltered our walk. The air was both ripe and fresh — full of life's yearning breath.

I felt dizzy and whole out there. Fully present and yet somehow set apart from my wife and kids. It was as if a curtain was pulled back. In those trees I saw a thrumming reminder of The Truth. The backseat arguments. Broken Goldfish crackers. Temporary tattoos flaking off in the foamy water of an evening bath. The first fresh feelings — hands clutched, breath short. Everything was there.

Every creature holds a string tied to the eternal. Every moment is a cousin of the creative force that formed our souls. This great love is what twines us all together. It is what makes the light possible. What helps us find the way home. It's the whole point of the story. The hope of the world.

The author — standing in awe of a giant redwood.
Trillium Falls Trail. Redwood National and State Parks.

I can still close my eyes and conjure the image of God I held in my head when I was a kid. I don't want to write too much about it because there's part of me that worries that if I write the description down in detail, the image in my head will be replaced by the words I've written and this picture I've called my own for forever will just sort of fade away. I don't want that to happen, even though I don't think what I saw in my head when I was little is what God really looks like. In fact, I don't think God *looks* like anything. What I mean is, you're not ever going to see God. Or hear or smell or taste or touch God. My bet is meeting God goes w-a-a-a-y beyond the human senses. Maybe *beyond* isn't the right word. It'll be *different*; let's just say that.

And I don't think heaven is a place you go to either. All those stories about clouds and gates, angels and robes — that's just made-up nonsense passed on to try to make people feel better about dying, or to scare people into behaving like they ought to behave anyway. I'm not trying to be sacrilegious or anything; it's just I understand how metaphors work.

I am not sure I know what a soul is either. Do you? Is it your true self? A fragment of being that ties you to whatever lies beyond? The collective flicker of the memories you hold most dear?

But I do know that out there in the trees one thing was certain: we are not just flesh, blood and bone. There *has* to be more. I'm not just saying that to make myself feel better either. I'm over all of that now.

Trillium Falls earned its name from the abundance of Western Trillium found on its rocky banks. Western Trillium or "Wake Robin," as it is sometimes called because of its association with early growth, is found in coniferous and mixed forests and produces a sweet, three-petaled flower each spring.

Emily Dickinson saw Hope as a songbird lifting her wings from a perch inside the soul. But to me, Hope is a forest flower yearning for light in the molasses shade of the Redwoods' understory. And when the magic happens, as it has for eons, Hope rewards the world with its petals. Glowing out of the darkness. It's a circle of becoming, beholding and being that hums of faith's mysteries.

By the time we arrived in August, the bloom of the Trilliums was a memory. Still, to stand with my family and bask in the presence of these common miracles was one of the greatest gifts of my life.

WHEN we returned to camp we ate our fill of hot dogs and macaroni and cheese. After the dishes were done we made our way to a steep path that leads down a dire drop-off to the roaring shore of the Pacific Ocean and a place called Agate Beach.

Agate Beach's sickle-shaped two miles of shore catches the Pacific's rip-tide blasts to powerful and stunning effects. It is a beautiful *and* fearful place. The lurking force of the undertow cautions even the most accomplished swimmer against getting in the water. So we walked along the edge of the tide and let the threat of waves wash over our ankles.

There were other campers there with us, combing the sand for the treasures that give the beach its name. As the sun sank into the horizon, we too gathered in a semi-circle and ran our fingers through the wash, stuffing our pockets with colorful, smooth stones — breadcrumbs that hopefully would some day lead us back to this moment.

Then Theresa and I watched together as the children returned to the water. Racing it forward and back. Casting shadows against a honeyed sky in the golden and dying light.

The Last Day in the Woods
(Day 17. Redwoods National Park)

ONE OF THE THINGS I love most about spending time out in the natural world is the implicit invitation you feel out there to ignore all of the stupid, meaningless trappings of society. It's easy to see that it doesn't really matter if you drive a Ford or a Lexus when you're standing next to a tree that was already old when Shakespeare spoke his first word. Suddenly the sneakers you paid $250 for because the website allowed you to individually design them seem painfully trivial and temporary. The Trail is The Chief Reminder that we are all created equally fallible. You're just another creature on this earth swimming in the soup of survival. And when you feel this, things fall into place, the proper perspective is restored. It's like waking up after a long and restful night's sleep.

WE set an alarm for only the second time on the trip so we could be sure to arrive at the visitor center in Orick before it opened. We wanted to be first in line to secure a permit to drive down six miles of dusty road to the head of a trail that descends 800 feet to the Tall Trees Grove — home to some of the tallest trees on planet Earth.

There is a locked gate at the top of the road. But if you are lucky enough to be among one of the fifty parties granted a permit to visit the grove each day, you are given a secret code which unlocks the gate and allows you to access the trees. Basically it's a gated nature community.

One of the main reasons our world is so messed up these days is people don't spend enough time out among the trees. They're too busy working in order to buy those $250 sneakers I mentioned before. I bet if everyone in America got the chance to hike through the Redwoods, there would be a whole lot less crazy shit going on. It follows that access to trails shouldn't be limited to the first fifty parties who show up each day. They should be open to everyone. This is America, right? Land of the free. Anyway, don't the tax dollars of regular Americans pay to maintain these trails and parks? How dare they throw a locked gate up in front of any of it?

My Grandpa Bindig was a cartoonist. Once his kids were grown, he turned one of their old bedrooms into a studio complete with shelves lined with comic books, a sprawling drafting board desk, and clunky wooden drawers filled with every art supply imaginable; from exacto-knives to goopy old bottles of rubber cement. The place smelled like imagination.

He decorated the walls of this magical room with favorite comic strips, awards he'd won, and grinning photos of himself standing next to the likes of Charles Shultz. Framed on one of the walls was a promotional poster, created in the early 1970s, of Walt Kelly's Pogo the Possum standing in a stew of scattered trash on the forest floor and looking forlornly out at his readers. The caption above Pogo reads: "We have met the enemy and he is us," a line first etched into the American consciousness by Master Commandant Oliver Perry in a letter written to future president and then Major General, William Henry Harrison during the War of 1812. Call it foreshadowing.

As stated, the mission of the National Park Service is: "... to [conserve] unimpaired the natural and cultural resources and values of the National Park System for the enjoyment, education, and inspiration of this and future generations." But what's become tragically apparent over the years is in order to conserve these wonders, the NPS has to limit access to them. For if left to our own devices, being the selfish invasive species we are, we humans would spray-paint our names (or worse) onto the canyon walls, leave all our empty beer bottles on the shore of a crystal lake, and walk away from the still-smoldering embers of a campfire trusting that someone else will stop them from burning down the whole forest. The man in the badge looking over our shoulder might feel like the Gestapo to some, but he is nevertheless sadly necessary. If creation isn't curated, pretty soon there won't be anything left to enjoy.

We need protection from *us*.

ALL of this is to say, as I approached the locked gate leading to the dirt road that descends to the Tall Trees Grove, permit and secret code in hand, and found the lock broken and the gate slightly open, I felt ... conflicted. I stood alone in front of the gate thinking all of the paradoxical things I've just written about. I stood there so long in fact that Theresa assumed something was wrong. I mean, something *was* wrong, but the something I was thinking about just then wasn't the something Theresa thought was stopping me from opening the gate. "Does the code not work? What's going on?"

"Yeah, Dad, what's taking so long?" Harper shouted from the back of the Sequoia. "Let's get m-o-o-o-ving!"

"Theresa, can you give me the number for the visitor center?" I shouted back. "I need to call and let them know that the lock is broken and the gate is open."

"What?"

I walked back to the car and leaned in the open window to grab my phone. "Yeah, the woods are open for everyone today."

Henry moaned, "Oh God, you mean we woke up at the crack of dawn for nothing?"

"That's right," I said. "But watch out if word gets out." Theresa gave me the number, and I called in the repair, feeling both like a good Boy Scout and a hooligan throwing Teddy Roosevelt under the bus. Then I climbed back behind the wheel and made the long drive down to the trailhead.

THE Grove Trail snakes through an amazing jungle of diverse trees — punctuated by vibrant greens of a thriving understory. It was hard to resist the temptation to constantly document the hike with pictures, but though I did take my fair share of shots of the kids clinging like the slipped skin of cicadas to the grooves of the redwood trunks, I mostly kept my phone's camera in my pocket. Theresa and I scrambled over switchbacks as Henry, Max and Harper sprinted ahead on their way down the slope to the grove of ancient trees at the bottom of the trail's loop.

By comparison to the trail, the grove that is home to the redwoods is flat and open. It's written that several of the trees scratch the sky at over 350 feet, or taller than the Statue of Liberty and its pedestal combined. Touching these creatures is something I will never forget — like holding the hand of my dying grandfather, or watching my daughter ride away from me for the first time on her bike.

The trek down proved to be decidedly exhausting so before we headed back up, we ate our lunch on the roots of the trees, and asked a charming elderly couple we ran into down there to snap a family photo with a giant as the backdrop. From our picnic spot we could see the early afternoon light breaking into a clearing a few hundred yards away. From what I had read, I knew there was a creek running through the area, so we decided to investigate, maybe give our feet a good soaking in the cool water before climbing back up the trail.

Careful to make note of landmarks, we left the blazed trail and climbed through the brush. What we found when we broke through the branches was both stunning and tragic.

A smooth stone vertebrae stretched out before us. It was carved into the landscape by the flow of Redwood Creek, whose waters typically serve as a highway for salmon as they make their way to their various habitats in the floodplain. But the sun-soaked stones bore almost no water that day. Just shallow shaded pools and puddles. The years-long drought that has gripped the West drained the creek of its majesty. It was a sight out of a post-apocalyptic movie. Blazing sun. Silence where the gurgling water ought to have filled the air. An eerie absence of life.

There's a reason rivers are so often used by writers as symbols for a journey or a path a person might take in life. Human history has taught us to come to flowing waters. As Maclean says, "Eventually all things merge into one, and a river runs through it." But what does it mean if the rivers stop flowing? What happens then to that which must merge? Where will we go without water?

As weak as it was, I couldn't bear to see my children standing there on the scorching rocks. It felt like I was looking into their future. A world made uninhabitable by the careless acts of humankind. They wanted to follow the water-worn path of the riverbed, but I insisted we turn back to the woods. I made like safety was my motivation — I didn't want to get lost too far off the trail — but really it was my heart I was worried about.

THOUGH we didn't run into more than a handful of people on our way back up to the trailhead, when we summited the trail and found the Sequoia parked in the shade where we left her, it looked like the parking lot was almost full. Immediately I wondered if my call about the open gate had prompted any action, so when I saw a park ranger milling about by the map station, I walked over to her and introduced myself.

Thankfully she confirmed that a service call was placed earlier in the day; if it hadn't been already, the gate would be fixed.

"In a way it's a shame all of the beauty has to be gated in, isn't it?" I asked.

She nodded gravely, "A necessary shame."

"You think visitors would destroy it otherwise? This place is so magical."

"I agree with you," she said. "It is magical, but if over twenty years as a Park Ranger has taught me anything, it's that you should never underestimate people's willingness to destroy beauty in the name of profit. That and just general carelessness. Selfishness too." She then spent the next twenty minutes or so giving my children a condensed history of the lumber trade in the Pacific NorthWest. She also told us about so-called conservation efforts to replant the harvested trees via airdropped seeds. Like most lessons about the environment these days, her words felt as hopeless as they were confusing. How could anyone justify acting so carelessly toward this sacred land? The actions she described felt like giving a toddler a brown-paper bag of broken glass and Legos and asking her to sort them out. Pain is inevitable and the reward totally not worth it. Any joy that might have been stored in our hearts from our lunch in the grove was fleeting by the time the ranger finished her story.

"Thank you," I said, extending her my hand. "These are hard things to hear, but important nevertheless."

"I'm glad you see it that way." There was a quiet desperation to her tone. Her words were more gruff than grateful. "Just make sure to think about this place when you vote."

THAT morning, before we left for the visitor center in Orick, the boys spotted a trail out of the campsite that led through some tall grass and spilled out onto the top of a small bluff looking over a jagged cliffside. Below, you could see a rubble of sea-tossed rocks on which rested a colony of seals. The boys begged me to let them climb down for a closer look, but with the Tall Trees permit as a handy excuse I pushed them off until later, promising that, "If we get back to camp in time, we'll do some more exploring in the evening."

But despite my manipulative planning, when we arrived back at our campsite in Patrick's Point, it was just after 4:00pm. There was plenty of time to squeeze a crazy climb in before dinner. And the boys hadn't forgotten about it either. Moreover, tired as she was, Theresa wasn't up for a battle. So when the boys asked if we could "check out the cliff" she said, "If it's okay with your Dad, it's okay with me."

"I want to come!" Harper shouted. To which I smiled and agreed, assuming, given the risk, Theresa would say no and put an end to this whole adventure.

"Okay, Harper," Theresa said, "Stick close to Dad." Then under her breath she said, "Thanks for doing this sweetie. I could really use a few minutes to myself. I'll make dinner while you guys go explore, how about that?"

So it was that I found myself making my way toward a seaside cliff, alternately shouting out warnings and directions to my fast moving boys while clutching the sweaty hand of my seven-year-old daughter, suddenly irrationally certain that at any moment a fierce mountain lion would jump out of the brush and attack us. Yep, looks like we will die out of earshot of anyone. Serves me right, I thought. I mean, how stupid to be climbing down an out-of-bounds unmarked trail when literally *all of the literature* I read about the place warned me *not* to do this exact thing.

Why the hell am I doing this?

Well, for one thing, I was sort of proud of my kids for wanting to try it. I'm not exaggerating when I say the climb looked both scary and difficult. If you set aside the fact that their frontal cortexes are not yet fully developed and, therefore, they don't truly understand risks or their consequences, you've gotta love kids who see that kind of thing and think, "Let's go!" instead of "Hell no!" I'm just saying, I know kids who are afraid to ride their scooters around the block because doing so means they have to figure out how to steer in a not-so straight line without falling over. Jesus. What the hell are *those* kids going to do when they're faced with a *real* challenge in life? But, proud as I was of my kids' hearty spirits, I really didn't want them to die on my watch.

As we approached the cliff, I peeled off my flannel and tied it around a rock.

"What are you doing, Dad?" Max asked.

"I'm leaving a trail so when we die the search party will know where to find our bodies." Ah, a new approach: scare them shitless.

"Dad, it's fine." The stubborn glint in Henry's eyes that told me this was happening with or without me.

I pulled off my hat and put it in my teeth. "Climb on my back, Harper. I'll carry you down."

"I can climb down by myself, Dad," Harper said. "I'm not a toddler. And why is your hat in your mouth? It makes it hard to hear what you're trying to say."

I spit out the hat. "I'm going to drop the hat half way down. I'm leaving a trail for the authorities. Remember."

"Come on, Dad!"

"Look, you guys, this is stupid. It's really dangerous. There's no safe way down. We're *not* doing this, okay. Sorry. I changed my mind."

"But you said we could. You *promised*." And suddenly I felt that if I said no to *this*, I'd be saying no to everything.

Harper, Max and Henry — tempting the frothy Pacific.
Patrick's Point State Park. Trinidad, California.

WE made our way down the rock face as if climbing down a ladder. If you saw us from the sea we would have appeared to be an inward facing totem pole with Henry at the top and me at the bottom.

On the shore, the tide was rapidly rising. The air was violent with splashing waves. Still, we could see the seals less than fifty yards away, bulky and brooding in sleek clusters on the boulders that rose out of the tide. The kids wanted to get closer, but the roaring waves prevented us. The ocean humbles even the bravest of spirits.

Each of us turned an ankle, caught a foot or slipped down onto a now-scraped knee as we made our way close to where the water frothed and foamed. Eventually, by collective stillness, we agreed to go no further, and stood for a silent moment looking out over the water toward the other side of the world.

AFTER a don't-tell-mom close call on the cliff, after gathering my hat and flannel, after taking a ribbing from the boys for being so dramatic, and after full body tick checks on the trail, we found our way back to camp. I ate my dinner with shaking hands, the reality of what could have happened flashing on constant repeat before my mind's eye. Each time it was someone else against the rocks. Each time a different hand slipping through mine. Each time another voice calling out as it was carried away by the tide.

By the time dinner was over, I had accepted the fact that the worst hadn't happened. And it wouldn't happen now either. We made it to the shore and back again.

It was terrifying.

It was beautiful.

I built a fire and silently listened as Theresa and the kids talked about going back home. Who would Harper have as a teacher? Would Rosie the dog still remember us? Did Grandpa do a good job of tending to the plants? How many days until the start of school?

They were excited to see their friends, sleep in their beds again, and ride their bikes around town. They told funny stories and laughed together at memories around mouthfuls of chocolate, melted marshmallows and grahams. They were happy.

Our adventure wasn't over yet. We had another stop before we reached the city and two days with Theresa's sister, Sarah, before we flew back home. Shadows from the fire danced over their faces. My wife. My children. Joyful to return to the world. Excited even, to resume again. But I couldn't help feeling something else too. Like something precious was slipping away. And there was nothing I could do to stop it.

It was our last day in the woods.

A Messy Kind of Wonderful
(Day 18. Patrick's Point — The Reese Ranch Retreat)

THE NEXT MORNING, I woke with the sun to a silence so all-consuming it pulled me from my sleeping bag to investigate its cause. Outside of the tent it seemed the world was beginning again. Dew hung from every pine needle. A light breeze brushed my face. The tide whispered silent secrets to the shore. The sun, blinking awake on the edge of the horizon, shined its fresh light in waffle patterns through the fine webbed canopy of the branches overhead.

From where I stood, it seemed like each path leading away from our campsite had been brushed footprint-free overnight. In the magic of the morning, I was certain those paths would lead me anywhere I wanted to go if only I could muster the courage to take them. So I wrote a quick note on a napkin and placed it under a rock in the middle of the picnic table then walked off into the woods alone.

Slipping. Slipping. Slipping.

When I first started teaching, I hung a sign over my office door that read, *Teach like a Champion Today*. In those heady times, I poured myself into every lesson. Every seat in class was occupied by the hope of the world. And when a knock came on the door at

3:00 p.m. — my bag packed, one arm already in my coat, I pulled two desks together, my back to the clock as I whispered to myself the final stanza from Richard Wilber's great poem, "It is always a matter, my darling / Of life and death, as I had forgotten. I wish / What I wished you before but harder," and settled into my chair to listen to the waiting young person with all of my heart.

But now sometimes when a boy raises his hand in class, I swear I know for certain what kind of car he'll drive when he's twenty-five. Or exactly at what age he'll get his first tattoo. And there's the girl who'll join a sorority in college. Despite what the books I teach tell her, she'll walk out of my room thinking that good husbands can't be found in libraries. That vacations with the kids to Myrtle Beach will only come from her willingness to press up against him at the bar. None of them will read poetry when they're older. None of them will look at the stars.

Slipping. Slipping. Slipping.

My blonde-haired boy who looks just like me used to stand patiently at the base of the stairs each morning, a book in his hand and hope in his heart, waiting for a moment together. Just our shared heat in a chair and a story to start the day. That was enough for him. "Hey Dad," Henry used to say tapping *The Prisoner of Azkaban* with his pudgy fingers, "Little Har? Wanna read a little Har before breakfast?" But now he mostly grunts awake just before noon, and stumbles toward his phone to check the status of his world and answer all of his snaps before saying hello to his father.

I wonder if every parent goes through this. Is this a necessary pain? For so many years you are the sun in your children's sky. Then clouds come in: sleepovers, travel sports, Instagram. And in the quiet moments when the air clears, you find you now exist in two separate skies. Yours cast in twilight. Theirs cast in dawn.

Slipping. Slipping. Slipping.

In the first picture I ever took of Theresa the wind pulled her long chestnut hair across her face. We climbed the rickety fire escape together, our feet flirting with the open sky, then leaned out into the open — our elbows resting on the same rail. Her eyes danced and smiled back at me. And I knew I would love her forever.

Now we argue about receipts. I get frustrated about how she sorts the wash. She mutters to herself as she walks to the car to run back to the grocery store to pick up the essential ingredient I somehow forgot off the list. And when we say "I love you," it is a different kind of love. A love grown in delivery rooms and funeral parlors and parent-teacher meetings. Its trunk is thick, its branches weighty, its leaves secured safely against the winds of time. You can hang a tire swing in a tree like this. But sometimes I miss the uncertainty of the seedling. The thrill of those early branches twisting toward the light.

I know nothing lasts forever. Nothing gold can stay. The bud gives way to the blossom, whose fruit is the harvest of our home. This is both how it *is* and how it *should* be. And I welcome it with an open heart.

I'm just so tired of feeling old and useless.

THE narrow trail I took away from our campsite curved into the dense brush. I answered the morning's stillness with a spoken prayer. "Let me see a bear," I said. This is my last morning in the woods. Let it walk slowly into the path in front of me and pause — just for a moment. Not startled, just aware. Let our eyes meet and our breath mingle. I'll stop and decide whether or not to run. I'll know just what to do. And she'll stop and size me up. Both of us standing still and watching. Then I'll know for sure the fate of all the things I wish for. When she huffs and turns away to walk off through the brush again in search of her morning meal, stray branches combing her fur as she goes, I'll feel something certain in the reprieve of her absence. A clearness will come. An assurance. A sign. That is what I was looking for as I walked through the woods alone that morning: a sign. A tangible emblem that everything now seemingly broken will come together again. That it'll all work out fine. But there was no bear in the woods that morning. Just the path before me, and the sound of my soft solitary steps walking through the dawn.

When I came back to our campsite forty-five minutes later, I found my family sitting around the table happily gobbling down oatmeal. All of their bags were already packed.

WHEN we had finally decided on the route of our trip, we knew that the drive from Redwoods to Theresa's sister's place in San Francisco was too long to tackle in one day - especially at the end of three weeks of driving. So we booked a night at the Reese Ranch Retreat in Witter Springs; roughly the halfway point between the woods and the bay. With that destination in mind we tucked our tent, camp stove, and sleeping pads forever into the trunk of the Sequoia, and pulled out of Patrick's Point headed for the Avenue of Giants.

THE Avenue of Giants is a winding, thirty-one mile route through southern Humboldt County. Though it runs side-by-side with the much-faster Route 101, we chose to take The Avenue because of its noted natural wonders and human curiosities.

Along the way we saw a sign for the trunk of a fallen redwood tree turned into a living room. The novelty of the notion compelled us to stop. Pulling off the road, we bought a ticket for the privilege of walking through the place. It probably took us longer to park than it did to marvel at the set up.

Down the road a bit there was another advertised tree-abode. We paid to see this one too because it promised to be a full house built into the trunk of a tree. Turns out, it was just two small circular rooms stacked on top of each other. I can't imagine how a person could make a living off of tending to such kitschy roadside attractions, but the people shelling out the tickets seemed happy enough. They take what the world gives them. Trying their best to get by.

Theresa decided to stave off the kids' disappointment about the falsely advertised grandeur of the place with early afternoon ice cream cones for everybody. Noble as their struggle for survival was, the thought of giving the proprietors of these places any more of my money did something funny to my appetite, so while Theresa and the kids waited in line next to the tree house's rear door, I decided to wait in the car. Sitting alone in the shade of the parking lot, I saw a sign for a marijuana dispensary attached to the side of the joint.

A friend gave me a dime bag and a fresh pipe for my fortieth birthday. I smoked alone while Theresa sat with me in the backyard trying her best to hide her disdain. According to her, a good healthy high wasn't worth the risk of the neighbors calling the cops or worse yet, our kids coming out to find mom and dad wasted by the fire. In the end, I was so out of practice that I half-choked to death that night and went to bed with my eyes burning and an oxygen-deprived headache. What's more, Theresa rolled over to face the wall before I even had a chance to turn out the light. Not so fun.

Still, they've got edibles now, and I guess it's legal out there in California, two facts that almost convinced me that getting high with my wife on a family vacation was a good call. So I got out of the car and stood there in line flirting with the idea of buying a bag full of yummy gummies to enjoy together around the campfire that night. I was one person away from the register when I heard a rapping on the window next to me. When I looked up and saw Harper's sweet, ice cream smeared face pressed against the glass, I ducked out of line and made my way back to the Sequoia. I answered Theresa's puzzled look with a shrug. "I was just *thinking* about it," I said. "I didn't *buy* anything." She uncrossed her arms as we pulled back onto the road. "Maybe next time though," I laughed. She didn't smile back.

We took a ten-minute detour off the road to pay eleven dollars for the right to drive through a rectangular hole carved into the base of a redwood tree. Even though I thought it was kind of stupid, I took a video of it on my phone. I hate small spaces, and the side of the tree was literally centimeters away from the folded-in side mirrors of the Sequoia. With the sunroof open, we could easily touch the top of the hole as we drove through. I wonder what would have happened if we got stuck? The folks who cut their way through the trunk clearly never imagined we'd ever make vehicles this big.

Unnerving as it was, I pulled around for a second spin through the tree, just so Theresa could snap a picture of it from the other side. In the photo, the car is half in and half out of the hole. Max is sitting on the roof in a way that causes a viewer to wonder how he ever made it through the hole intact. Harper is smiling and leaning out of the passenger side window to similar effect. Henry is in the back rolling his eyes, but you can't see him in the photo. I, looking very much like Clark Griswold, am leaning out of the driver's side window with a curved left arm reaching up to the sky, a shit-eating grin on my face.

Kitsch has a way of rubbing itself off on you.

The Bindig family & The Sequoia — making their way through the Chandelier Drive-Thru Tree. Leggett, California.

IT was just after four in the afternoon when we pulled into Reese Ranch Retreat. The Ranch sits in the bottom of a bowl of mountains. There we found a bright red barn with chickens milling about beside it. A wide-open blue sky domed over a sprawling horse pasture. Beside the villa whose high ceilings and broad windows made a sanctuary of the clouds, a trio of goats called playfully to us. Even now Harper will tell you their names: Casper, Brown Sugar and S'mores. We found the key with the welcome note and made our way inside. It was as if we stepped back in time.

Before turning down the road to the ranch, we stopped at a general store and bought a couple of frozen pizzas, a bag of carrots and a box of ice cream sandwiches. So while the pizzas baked, we toured the grounds together taking in the cinematic openness of its wide-screen beauty. We met the spacious silence with a stillness of our own.

After dinner each of us took a long shower. Then Theresa set up the beds and I cleaned up the kitchen. When all that was done we built a fire together in the growing twilight, while the kids binged on bad TV and ice cream. Soon the flames were roaring and the night was spackled with stars. We sat together in the breezy darkness looking up at the velvet sky.

One by one the kids gave up the glow of the TV to join us by the fire. We sat in a semi circle in red metal rocking chairs and talked with casual closeness deep into the night.

AFTER I doused the fire with a hose and the kids climbed into bed, Theresa and I turned down the lights and crawled into each other's arms — alone at last. Later when I closed my eyes and gave myself up to the dreams of the day, I found myself racing again along The Avenue of Giants. In my mind we twisted our way through the wind-whipped trail of trees as it curved for mile after shady mile in the dappled light. Humming along with the windows open, my hand darted up and down in the breeze, my eyes full of shade and wonder. And as I lay there half-awake, I felt this profound sense of gratitude for humankind settle over me. Gratitude for the humans who thought to carve a road through the trees so I could drive on it. For the people who settled this land and built this ranch so we could have a place to stay. For everyone.

It's easy to be cynical. People do a lot of stupid, selfish, shitty things. But sometimes if you look close enough, and if you can find a way to ignore the worst actors, you'll suddenly see that most of humanity is really just a messy kind of wonderful. A mixed-up sacred stew of hopes and dreams and possibilities. Each one of us striving for what we think is the light. Kind of like the forest floor in a way, only somewhat less organic. Only in this case, somewhat less pure.

Lilacs and Hand Grenades
(Day 19. The Reese Ranch Retreat — Millbrae, California)

It feels almost impossible to experience silence these days. I'm talking about true lasting silence. There is always noise. The thermostat kicking on in the middle of a winter night. The air conditioner. The fan in the bathroom. The busy bustling of school buses passing by on a cool October morning. The ping, vibration, or badge-flash of my phone. The nagging dread of the newspaper. The email inbox. The voices in my head.

It's the voices I find most troubling.

I want to be clear, I don't actually hear voices. I'm not *crazy* or anything. It's more like a running soundtrack of thoughts. Thoughts I struggle to shut off.

They start first thing most mornings, sometimes even before I open my eyes, and almost always before I get out of bed. My mind goes to something: a conversation from the day before, an anticipated meeting, or some interaction that happened while I was coaching my kids. And then it's just wash and repeat. Wash and repeat. And I'm not just thinking about stuff either. I'm *analyzing* it. Dissecting it. Probing for a weakness or some kind of flaw. And when I find one, that's when my inner critic pounces. That's when the real fun begins.

When I was younger, I was a really healthy, happy kid. But when my mom went back to graduate school, and my father's work responsibilities picked up, my brother and I were left on our own a lot. That first year I must have gained nearly thirty pounds. I was dieting by the time I was in third grade. Weight Watchers pizzas for dinner. Drawn up exercise plans. Reduced portions at breakfast. Food became fodder for self-loathing. I was at battle with my body. And the near constant body shaming imposed upon me by my older brother certainly didn't help any. He'd skip down the stairs to get ready for cross-country practice, making sure that everyone in the room noticed the sickening slap of my flabby thighs, when I followed him. He called me "Whubba," pointed out spots of cellulite on my hips whenever I pulled my shirt off at the beach, and scoffed that my choice of sports was really just an excuse to be fat. I can't remember a time after fifth grade that I felt 100% comfortable in my body. I grew up knowing that, when it came to me, there was always work to do. Always something to criticize.

Then again maybe this inner-critic is just a remnant of my football days. I was a player who was deeply motivated by criticism, constructive or otherwise. The first thing I did every single time I walked into my college locker room was check the depth chart — even after I was well established as the starter at my position. I never wanted to take for granted that I earned my spot. After all, a successful athlete never settles for his past best because first you settle, then you slip. I trained myself to never feel content. Never take the deep, celebratory breath of "good enough." You can always get better, right? I needed to feel the hunger of the hunted.

Over nine formative years of playing football, I was conditioned to live with a constant set of ever-changing goals in mind. It was the only way I knew how to be. So when the last whistle blew and I was done playing, I scaled-down my weight room sessions and started running for exercise instead with the goal of completing a marathon in mind.

I dropped down to pre-high school weight and cranked out endless miles. In the ten years after college, I successfully completed four marathons, breaking the four-hour mark in my last one. But even when I was cruising at my fastest pace, even when the mirror showed a body transformed from nose guard to runner, all I saw were the flaws. And whatever peace I gained from the hours of sweaty solitude was instantly forfeited with a glance at my watch. Running can be like that. Every step is an invitation to push harder. That's one of the things I like about it.

What's weird is, for a long time I didn't recognize my constant self-criticism as a problem. It's just what I knew. Feedback is the breakfast of champions. My crabby inner critic was just coaching me up. And it worked too. I've accomplished a lot of great things in my life. But shortly after I turned forty, something seemed to shift.

With all of the kids in school full-time, Theresa started kicking up her work engagement. While we waited for her shift to a private nutritional-counseling practice to gain traction, it was still somewhat necessary for me to hold down a couple of gigs in order to make ends meet. I was teaching full-time, coaching my kids, working a couple of evenings a week as an adjunct instructor at a local community college, and grinding through separate stacks of essays at night as part of a college consulting team. This on top of trying to read bedtime stories, throw the ball in the backyard, and go for long bike rides with my kids. I needed the most I could muster out of every possible minute just to survive the grind. I felt like if I relaxed, even for a second, something important wouldn't get done. I *had to* stay busy.

It became increasingly harder and harder to wake up each morning and crank out long runs and weight-lifting sessions. I was always tired. Still as the pounds piled back on, each night I'd give myself a pep talk as I set the alarm. Promising tomorrow would be different. Tomorrow I'd make some time for myself. Write. Read. Run. Get back out into nature. Get back into the groove. But by the next morning, getting out of bed felt impossible again. So I'd hit the snooze button and lay half-awake listening as my inner-critic tried to jeer me into my running shoes.

"Get up you fat piece of shit! Excellence is not a sometimes thing! How fucking hard is this? It doesn't matter how fast you go. Get up! Nothing is going to get better while you lay in this fucking bed!" Sometimes it worked and sometimes it didn't.

Soon, even the little things began to feel hard. Watering the houseplants on a Saturday morning felt like an intolerable burden. I'd get pissed, I mean *really* angry, when one of my kids left their wet towel on their bedroom floor. And God forbid some dinner dish get left to soak in the sink overnight. That crusted pan in the sink the next morning felt like a personal affront.

Each time I read the newspaper it felt like I was at war with the world. Everyone and everything was screaming at me. It was like I was living in this state of strobe-light stress. And there was nothing I could do to escape it.

It wasn't a conscious decision or anything like that, but somewhere along the line I started drinking a whole lot more. I felt like getting buzzed and blurry was the only way to turn things off. The only way to feel even sort of normal. But while alcohol certainly made some moments feel more tolerable, on the whole it made everything a whole lot worse. When your life already feels like a struggle, a hangover has a way of making the next day feel like a tour of hell. Soon, like everything else, my drinking felt out of control. I struggled to stop.

I knew I needed help, but as a guy used to managing things by myself, it felt weak to talk about this with anybody. I mean, weren't all of my friends in the same soup? Complaining wasn't going to change anything. Besides, every time I talked to Theresa about it I ended up feeling like I was just another problem for her to solve. Nobody wants to be somebody else's problem. No, I just needed to put my head down and plow through it. That's what always worked before. But this time everything felt so heavy and impossible. I just wanted it all to stop. Pretty soon a new refrain started running through my head.

"If this is what life is like now, then maybe I don't want to be living it. Maybe everybody would be better off without me."

THE difference between how I felt at my life's lowest point — before a semester off from school, before I gave up my second and third jobs, before therapy, and a good break from the bottle — and how I felt when I woke to the silent sun shining through the broad open windows of Reese Ranch was like the difference between lilacs and hand grenades. And I felt that difference palpably.

I knew by evening we'd be back in the world; gathered with my sisters-in-law and their families for a few days together in one of California's biggest cities, our family's solo adventure on The Trail all but over. But what I was most focused on right then was the rise and fall of my chest. Right then in the silence of the morning

I was acutely alive. There was nothing else. No voices in my head. No schedules to review. No news of the world. There was nothing but the sweet here and now. Ripe and ready to begin again.

WHEN the others finally stirred awake, we ate our breakfast next to the horse pasture then took our time packing up. I signed the guest registry and left the last copy of my novel I brought along on the trip as a gift for Catherine, the purveyor and visionary creator of the Reese Ranch Retreat. Then we locked up the villa and headed to the car.

I paused alone outside of the Sequoia with my hands in my pockets, soaking in the sunny silence before climbing in for our last long day of driving. There were chickens at my feet and an impossibly blue-sky overhead.

I knew then that this moment was just as good as any we had. And maybe that was the secret I'd been chasing all along. There is sanctity in every second. God, forgive me for ever wishing this away.

Harper — basking in the glow of the morning sun. Reese Ranch Retreat. Witter Springs, California.

WE set our course along the Russian River through Northern California's wine country and eventually decided to go out of our way to stop at the Fort Ross winery, just outside of Jenner. For an hour Theresa and I sipped wine together while we forced our three road-weary children to sit off to the side, in the bar's overstuffed leather chairs, sifting silently through brochures and *Wine Enthusiast* magazines under the threat of instant death if they made so much as even a little sound. I know that sounds a bit like child abuse, but sometimes you have to go to extreme measures to keep your marriage alive and well.

Driving along the coast with a box of clinking bottles in the back, we made our way to Theresa's sister Sarah's place in Millbrae. We arrived just before dinner. It felt like a lifetime since we were last there, but really it was just over two weeks. A slanted figure eight loop through three states. Just over 3,700 miles. And the memories. The memories.

WE didn't plan it this way, but Theresa's older sister Cathy, her husband Ed, and their three children flew into San Francisco that night as well — on their way home to Boston from a trip to Hawaii to celebrate Ed's parents' fiftieth wedding anniversary. So as we dug into our pulled pork sandwiches, a decidedly celebratory Thanksgiving mood swept through the family group.

Soon the wine was flowing freely, Cathy's college-aged daughters were ribbing each other in the mostly-fun way of siblings, and Ed was holding court — telling an array of funny stories from their trip to the islands. It was a loud and joyful table. Though I wanted to join in the revelry, I felt myself withdrawing as the night grew late. Was I just tired or was it something else?

Once everything was cleaned up and Cathy's family was getting ready to head to the apartment they were renting for the night, I asked the crowd if any of them wanted to get up early the next morning and run across the Golden Gate Bridge with me. I knew we planned to spend the day doing a touristy loop through San Francisco, and running across the bridge seemed like a good way to kick things off. Plus it was once a destination-goal of mine, back when I was putting in a lot of running miles.

Even though across-the-bridge-and-back is a relatively short run, I knew Theresa and the kids weren't going to do it with me, and with her husband Greg out of town, Sarah had her hands full with getting her three children ready for the day. But Cathy played both soccer and lacrosse in college and still held some high school track records. She's one of the most natural athletes I know. Ed rowed crew at Dartmouth and is known for taking frequent, exercise-themed trips with his old college pals. Some dudes go on benders with their buddies to away-NFL stadiums, crew guys go for twenty-four hour hikes in the mountains. Caitlin played club lacrosse at Syracuse, Morgan rowed for BC and going into his junior year of high school, Hudson was slated to play three varsity sports. Surely some of this bunch would join me.

But whether it was the wine or their jet-weary legs, all but Ed brushed off the suggestion as crazy. So as Ed hustled out the door, we made quick plans for a 6:00 a.m. foggy morning run together.

ONCE the kids were tucked in with their cousins, Theresa and I crashed together in the side room we shared for the night. Though we held hands as she drifted off to sleep, I felt far away from her now. When we had pulled into Sarah's driveway, everyone burst from the car to a crowd of hugs and bags being carried in. I don't know why, but something about the easy exit from our trip's chariot felt weird to me. I'm not sure what I was looking for. Maybe a moment there, with the car forever in park, and all of us still strapped in together, where we all looked at each other and shared a *we-did-it-family!* smile. But there was none of that. Just hustling on to the next thing.

FORTY minutes later my phone buzzed awake with a message from Ed. Cathy and the kids would be joining us on our run. Happy for the company, my head heavy with wine and swirling with the weight of re-entry, I closed my eyes again and fell into a fitful sleep.

When my alarm woke me up at 5:30 a.m. the next morning, I was dreaming of lilacs.

Something In Between
(*Days 20 and 21. Millbrae, San Francisco and Palo Alto, California*)

THE SIX OF US: Ed, Cathy, Caitlin, Morgan, Hudson and I, crammed into their rental car and made our way, at 6:30 a.m., to the parking lot adjacent to The Golden Gate Bridge. For a moment there, as we idled in the early morning traffic, it occurred to me that my somewhat sullen and separate mood, along with the leading role I played in finishing off the available wine the night before, must have prompted a family awakening to "Uncle Matt's" state of being, thus the Smith clan's late night change of heart. Maybe this so-called "early-morning run" was really just a ruse to get me to some padded room where the whole of my extended family would be waiting, along with a team of well-paid therapists, to tell me in no uncertain terms that it was time to get my shit together before locking me away in a clinic against my will. But as the bridge came into sight it seemed another sort of intervention was more likely.

"Keep in mind, you guys," I said as we got out of the car, "I'm really out of shape." No one responded. "Like *really*. I mean I don't mind *at all* if you guys run ahead. I'll just see you on the other side."

"But you've run *marathons*, Uncle Matt," Caitlin laughed. When she was a little girl, she baked me a cake with the frosted word "Finish," across its crown to match the shirt I wore when I ran The Boston Marathon. "This is only like, what, three, maybe four miles total?"

"Yeah, you got this, Uncle Matt." Hudson cuffed my shoulder. "I'll stay with you. Don't worry."

"And, I haven't run in like two weeks," Morgan said. Then she set off in front of the group at a brisk 7:00 minute mile pace. "I'll be happy to make it to the other side," she laughed over her shoulder.

The group mostly hung together as we made our way past, cars, bikers, walkers and fellow runners buzzing by in the shadow of the swinging cables (at least it felt like they were swinging to me). But when we reached the halfway point our group began to naturally spread apart as each of us fell into our own running rhythms.

Ed was nice enough to film the scene: his family cruising along smiling and waving, me laboring to not digest myself, looking at the bridge's suicide nets and wondering about my options as I tried to not fall too far behind. Seriously. It was bad.

When it was over, we made our way down a series of steps to a ragged, semi-paved beach. We waded out into the waters of The Golden Gate Strait and, trading salt for salt, washed off the morning run in a vein of the Pacific. Then we drove to a nearby café to meet up with Theresa and Sarah and all of the other kids for a quick breakfast and tour-planning session.

There were definitely some things I really wanted to do that day, but over the years I've learned it's best, in such cases, to appreciate my role as an in-law and make my requests in private to Theresa. Then just sit back and let whatever happens, happen. A cork on a stormy sea. That's me. Easier said than done, for sure.

Ed must have had the same idea because he slid into the booth next to me and arched an eyebrow in the direction of the next booth where Cathy, Sarah and Theresa sat poking at the maps on their phones. As I ate my muffin, washed down with a large black coffee, he handed me a tissue-paper wrapped magnet. *I ran across The Golden Gate Bridge* it proudly proclaimed. "Nice work, Uncle Matt," he said. "No way would my family have done that without you." Gotta love the guy.

Max — offering up his support.
Crissy Field East Beach. San Francisco, California.

JUST before we stopped for lunch, after wandering around Fisherman's Wharf and snapping distant pictures of Alcatraz, we encountered a homeless guy holding up a sign that read, "I need weed. b.t.w. Fuck Trump!" To my horror, Henry snapped his picture.

"What the hell are you doing?" I barked, "This isn't the zoo. That person isn't there for your amusement."

"Sorry. God. I just thought his sign was funny," he said, disgusted and embarrassed by my overreaction. "I just wanted to send a picture of it to my friends."

"You *may not* send that picture to your friends. In fact, give me your phone for the next hour. This is ridiculous." Henry muttered to himself, but nevertheless did what he was told. Then he skipped away to catch up with his cousins.

As I stood watching my son walk away, I couldn't help thinking that a twenty-minute conversation with this homeless guy would probably teach both Henry and me a whole lot more about San Francisco than a visit to Pier 39, which was where we were heading next. But to learn what a homeless guy has to teach you, first you've got to notice him — not just notice him, but really *think* about him. Talk to him. *See* him. And most people don't want to do that. And maybe they're right. I mean, maybe the homeless guy is just a deranged drug addict. Maybe it's better just to skip along the surface. Maybe the safe summary is best. That way, worst case you end up with a bunch of cool pictures on your phone.

PIER 39 is a tourist-packed strip of commercial real estate at the edge of Fisherman's Wharf. It is ripe with plentiful shopping opportunities, gaudy attractions like a two-story carousel, and man-made distractions like video arcades. There's an aquarium there too, but if you're really into checking out the native wildlife all you need to do is head to the actual pier (versus the shopping strip named after it), where you'll be able watch the sea lions haul themselves out of the bay and onto the floating docks, which according to local legend they began occupying back in 1989 in response to the Loma Prieta earthquake. The juxtaposition between the sea lions' struggle to find a safe place in an increasingly hostile and shrinking habitat and the busy buzz of the commercial center struck me as an ironic tableau of our world's battle lines. Which one of these two forces will win out in the end? As I turned my attention to the water, the soundtrack of the scene seemed to offer an answer.

Docked nearby was a large commercial cargo shipping boat whose sturdy sides were apparently due for a good washing. As the sun broke through the clouds and the day's heat settled in, the pounding of the power-washers drowned out not only my attempts at conversation with my nephews, but also all other thoughts. There was nothing to do but to sit with my family, stuffed close together with strangers, eating $100 worth of processed food off of plastic trays, and watch as a shipping boat loaded to the brim with goods, got a power-washed bath in preparation for its next trip across the ocean. The ear-splitting madness of it all made the desert, the mountains, the trees and the tide all feel very far away.

AFTER lunch, while Theresa and her sisters herded the kids forward on foot, Ed and I jogged back to where we parked the cars that morning and drove them to a garage in the heart of Chinatown. Then we took a cab to meet everyone so we could climb the fabled streets of the city together. Poking through shops we'd never find in Buffalo and navigating the packed cityscape, my kids got to explore a place unlike any they'd seen before.

Later, like true tourists, we hung off the back of trolley cars and peppered the driver with dorky questions about the best part of his job. "Every once in a while," he said, "I'll get to drive someone who's really excited about visiting San Francisco."

"I'm really excited about visiting San Francisco," Harper said, dangling her legs outside of the trolley as it crept up the impossibly steep incline of the crowded street. The driver just laughed and laughed.

Cathy's kids eventually peeled off to do some shopping on their own and Sarah took one of the cars home to get started on the meal. There were a few more spots I wanted to see, so my family and I, along with Cathy and Ed, soldiered on into the late afternoon haze — our eyes on the corner of Haight and Ashbury streets and the house where the Grateful Dead were living when they got busted during the Summer of Love.

Throughout the day, we traveled mostly on foot. When we finally sat down for dinner, somebody's smart watch said we walked more than twelve miles. It felt like it too. Everyone was a bit wilted. But after the food was passed around the table, spirits rose as we recounted our favorite parts of the day. Before long our gathering was transformed into a rollicking recollection full of laughs and stories.

As I worked with Theresa to clear the table and do the dishes, my phone buzzed awake with a series of texts from the varsity basketball coach asking if I would ever consider taking on the task of coaching Henry's 7th and 8th grade team. I'd coached this group before with some success, but I wasn't sure if I wanted to add that back to my plate. Still, his text started an itch. As the evening wore on, with my family sitting around the table laughing at tall tales from the road, my mind kept swimming with potential line-ups and practice plans. Thoughts which came rushing back into my head again later as I lay next to my sleeping wife.

Late that night, after Cathy's family said their final good-byes ahead of their very early morning flight back to Boston and we pried the kids away from the TV and got them settled in their beds, I found myself sitting awake in the otherwise dark and sleeping house, alternating between reading the online edition of *The New York Times* and trying to figure out a balanced approach to playing time for the basketball team I hadn't even agreed to coach yet. Sometime after 3:00 a.m., sick to my stomach, I finally shut off my phone. I couldn't believe how quickly the world came rushing back in. It seems there's no escaping it. It seems there's no way out.

Theresa — riding the rails. Chinatown. San Francisco, California.

THE next morning, after spending a few lazy hours visiting the grounds of Toby's school, and once again stopping at Jamba Juice for an overpriced morning treat, Sarah and her kids joined us for a drive up to Stanford University, where we spent several hours wandering around the campus on a self-guided tour. We ate a packed picnic lunch, threw the football and frisbee back and forth across wide lawns of open grass, and snapped family photos with amazing architecture as their backdrop.

Late in our stay, I excused myself to find a restroom and instead wandered into a building full of offices for professors in the English department. Sure that no one was looking, I read the list of names on the office doors and imagined for a moment a different life for myself. What if instead of getting married and starting my high school teaching career, I had continued with my studies beyond Hobart and Harvard? Could I have ended up here? Closing that door once again, like so many others before it, I left the building without looking back.

I finally found my family again standing in a rough circle in the blazing sun of Stanford's main quad, collectively reading the etched plaque that explains the six haunting statues of the Burghers of Calais. Here's the passage:

> *In 1884 the French City of Calais commissioned Auguste Rodin to create a memorial honoring heroes of the Hundred Years' War. He depicted the six burghers, or citizens, who in 1347 volunteered to leave the defeated city barefoot, tied by rope at the neck, and offer their own lives and the keys to Calais to King Edward III of England. The burghers' fortitude, determination, and devotion to their community preserved Calais from being pillaged at the end of a devastating siege . . .*

> *For Rodin this episode was an opportunity to celebrate the idea that heroic deeds may be performed by ordinary people. He did not follow tradition by idealizing the figures, rather he was uncompromising in his depiction of the emaciated hostages and represented them as distinct individuals. Their faltering steps, despairing gestures, and anguished expressions eloquently express the inner turmoil of each man struggling in his conscience between fear of dying and devotion to their cause.*

As I walked among the six figures absorbing their pain and conflict, haunted by the impossibility of their still-stoic postures, my mind found its way back to my favorite lines from Shakespeare.

On the battlefield as the men wait to confront the usurping King, Ross brings news to Macduff of his family's ruthless slaughter. After watching his comrade initially falter through grief and denial, Malcom exhorts him to "Dispute it like a man." To which Macduff replies, "I shall do so / But I also must feel it as a man." To be fully human. To *feel* the sting of the world's pain. This must come first.

I've always loved this scene because it represents a striking rebuke of the notion that there is somehow a direct relationship between the denial of one's emotions and toughness. There is much to be admired about a willingness to go on, without complaint or acknowledgement, in the face of *physical* pain. Ignoring your body's call to STOP! in the name of achieving a certain end takes both courage and a kind of rugged grace. I certainly admire that. But the idea that it is somehow noble or tough to ignore one's feelings, to bury them away, not speak of them, seems totally counter-intuitive to me. It's *hard* to feel things fully and go on trying anyway. Yet everybody, boys especially, are always taught that emotions are for the weak. Crying at movies is for pussies, and all that other bullshit. You can go ahead and add that to the list of things society gets stupidly wrong.

Maybe this is why, of all the things I saw over the two days we spent with Sarah and her family at the end of our trip, it's the Burghers of Calais that affected me the most.

Each of the men is so clearly broken, yet still so certainly strong. They are humbled by their circumstances, ropes around their necks, vulnerable to collapse; yet their eyes are clear through the anguish. They are standing all the same. Striving, against the odds, to finish their story with honor on their minds and hope in their hearts. If I could only do the same.

WHAT'S weird is even though I spent nearly every waking minute of our days in Millbrae and San Francisco with my wife and kids, I have almost no memories of interacting with any of them. It's almost like we weren't together — like I was walking through the world alone.

I finished the packing in time to help a bit with dinner and its cleanup. When it grew dark we all gathered around the TV to watch *Won't You Be My Neighbor*, a documentary about Mr. Rogers. I know, right, not exactly the film you'd expect for a thirteen, ten and seven year old. Honestly, though, I think the kids would have watched two hours of lawn growing footage at that point, so desperate were they for the chance to sit in front of a screen and chill. And for some reason, all of the adults in the room insisted on this film. Maybe because sometimes it's nice to be reminded that there's a different way to live. I know I take courage from that.

We went to bed shortly after the movie ended. We had another long day of traveling ahead. Soon we'd be back home again. Maybe some part of each of us would be changed by what we experienced on the trip. Maybe nothing would change at all. Maybe it was something in between. Either way, the world was waiting for us. We needed our rest.

The Reset Button
(Afterword)

. . . IT'S WEIRD BEING "BACK in the world." I find myself less sure, driven to consume, to keep up. Judging myself (body, choices, abilities), contaminated with the flow of society (news cycle) . . . I felt totally different "on the trail". More focused on the gifts, the beauty, my life.
— Excerpt from the final journal entry of the trip. Wednesday, August 21, 2019.

A month before his eleventh birthday, Max asked if he could have a sleepover to celebrate with his friends. I absolutely *hate* hosting sleepovers, but this would be Max's first, so we agreed. We set about making plans for his birthday weekend, but because so many of his friends are involved in travel sports and other activities, we needed to be flexible with the date. In the end, the only weekend that worked, within a month on either side of his birthday was the first weekend of March.

The boys started their night together by attending a middle school dance at the Boys and Girls Club then returned to our house for pizza and ice cream (each boy got to pick his own pint of Ben and Jerry's). Normally we do not allow our kids to play video games at home, but on rare occasions I will dig out my old

Nintendo gaming system and set it up for a few rounds of Super Mario Brothers, Tetris or Tecmo Bowl. Max begged me to set it up for when they got home from the dance, so I crawled up into the attic and brought down the box of cords and game cartridges. Once all the pizza and ice cream were gobbled up, the guys piled together in the living room for a long night of marathon TV watching, potato chip eating, and video games.

At some point before I went to bed, Luke, one of Max's friends, challenged me to a Tetris battle. I'm rightfully rusty at Tetris, but I still managed to clear 93 lines. When Luke started playing he made a few false moves and the lines started quickly stacking up toward the top of the screen. Before I really knew what was happening, Luke flicked his wrist forward and hit the reset button. The game started over.

"Hey, what was that?" I asked.

"I just reset it. I got a couple of bad lines."

"Right, so you lose," I said. "You can't just reset the game because it isn't going your way."

"Yeah you can," he shrugged. "It's like a do-over."

"But that means I won. I didn't get a do-over."

"That's because you didn't need to. You finished the game."

"But if you reset before the game finishes, you can just keep on playing until you win."

"Dad, Dad, it's cool," Max said. "Just let him play. You'll see."

"Okay," I said. "But I still don't see how it's fair."

"It *is* fair Mr. Bindig. It's all about the reset. You'll see." And eventually, I did see. I saw Luke rack up 107 lines on his way to a proclaimed victory over me in our Tetris battle. Total bullshit.

THE next Friday two senior boys walked into my classroom just after the bell rang for the last period of the day on the last day of a long week, and plopped themselves down in the two comfy armchairs I garbage-picked for my classroom earlier in the fall. Alternative seating, they call it. It's a thing in education these days. Gives the classroom a homier feel. Makes the kids feel more at ease. Kids are pretty stressed out these days. Every little bit helps.

Phil and Dave (not their real names), who were both all-stars in the school's vocational training program but sometimes struggled in their other academic classes, were in the process of figuring out how to secure a healthy supply of alcohol to take with them to the upcoming St. Patrick's Day parade in downtown Buffalo and weren't about to let a silly thing like the beginning of Sports Literature class derail the flow of their conversation. Phil slung his leg over the arm of the chair and took a long pull from the two-liter bottle of Coke he was carrying with him before passing it to Dave who eagerly followed suit.

I taught both of these boys during their junior year and grew to appreciate their quirks. Both of them were fairly capable thinkers; they just didn't "do" school. Homework? Reading? Writing essays outside of school hours? Nope. They just weren't going to do these things. The trouble is, you kind of *have* to do these things if you want to pass high school English class, which against all odds both of them did the previous year.

The fact that I spent a full academic year trying to convince, with moderate success, these boys that they weren't dumbasses just because they took Auto Tech, and that the real reason they always did poorly in school was because they didn't really know how to play the school game, won me a measure of their respect. Not that they ever said this to me; they just signed up for both of the senior English electives I was teaching the following year and slapped hands with me by way of greeting when they walked into class on the first day. It takes all kinds.

Most years by March, I tend to loosen the classroom discipline reins a little bit, especially with seniors, so it wasn't a big deal to me that they were a few seconds late to class nor that they didn't bother to apologize for it. They were just being self-absorbed teenagers. I didn't even care that they continued making their illegal plans after the bell rang; sometimes it takes me a few minutes to get the attendance recorded or pass out late papers before class officially starts. I think of those first few minutes as slush time anyway. No, the thing that really pissed me off was the fact that they were slurping from a shared two-liter bottle of Coke.

"Boys, what the hell are you doing?"

"What? Or yeah, sorry we were late. Do you want us to go get a pass?"

"No. The Coke is what I mean."

"I thought you said we could eat in here. Remember I don't get lunch because I come right from Auto?"

"You're sharing the Coke, Dave. That's the problem. Didn't you see all the signs in the hall about hygiene and what not? You know the *highly contagious* virus that everybody is talking about spreading around the United States?"

Phil stood up. "Mr. Bindig, I respect you and all, but this whole virus thing is just a load of crap. It's just the libs trying to make Trump look bad. The libs and China. You'll see. It's nothing. Pretty soon the whole thing will blow over and all those jerks will look stupid again. Just like the last election."

As I opened my mouth to tell Phil that the nonsensical drivel he just spewed was not only stupid but also irresponsible, the loud speaker crackled to life and the principal cleared his throat.

"Okay, guys, I'm sure you have all heard the rumors flying all around about the virus. We don't have any new information to share right now, but it looks like we might be shutting down for a few days at the beginning of next week . . ." the class burst into a round of applause and giddy chatter.

"Listen up!" I shouted. The room fell silent as the principal went on.

"For now, it's best for you to take all of your stuff home. That's everything out of your locker. Gym locker, whatever. Make sure to bring home your Chromebook and your charger too, just in case these few days turn into something longer. Okay, everybody, that's it for me. Stay Safe."

When the principal stopped talking I looked out at my class for a beat and said. "Hey, Phil."

"Yeah, what?"

"Put away the Coke."

FRIDAY, March 13, 2020. The last day of normal. Just a week more and it would have been seven months to the day from when we returned from our trip.

IF I'm being totally honest, one of the reasons I wanted to take this trip out West was because I was hoping to hit the reset button on my life. To start over. Clean the slate.

Before we started out, my life felt cluttered and out of control. Like I was just a vessel, along for the ride on a rollercoaster that made me sick. More and more I was bogged down by the latest tragedy in the headlines, the mindless minutiae at work, the cattiness of my colleagues, the natural growing distance between my kids and me, and the stress put on my marriage by the constant shuffling of schedules. I just wanted it all to stop.

And for about three weeks in the summer of 2019, it did. And I will always be grateful for that.

Theresa and Harper — searching for lost treasure. Agate Beach. Patrick's Point State Park. Trinidad, California.

ONE morning in early April 2020, Theresa and I sat down together and erased nearly everything from our calendar. All at once I felt sad, horrified, thrilled and free. The inertia of life dictates so much of how we spend our days. But that was all over now. What was once a colored jigsaw puzzle picture of frazzled and full lives, became a white screen of opportunity.

THE first COVID spring turned into a summer of racial reckoning, madness returned to the streets. When my children huddled with their friends at a roadside protest, masked and earnest and holding handmade signs crying out for justice and equality, they were threatened and sworn at. Later a total stranger driving by in a truck called my wife a "fucking cunt" as she sat on our porch drinking her morning tea, just because of the sign in our yard. And the Redwoods in California burned by the acre as never before.

The fall brought a curtain of hatred down over our country. Fights in schools about masks and distancing measures. Mobile morgues. Kids home and helplessly trying to learn from a screen. A contested election. Lies and deceit. Holidays spent in isolation. Then a horde of lethal traitors, killing cops and storming the Capital Building to overturn an election that didn't go their way.

A few months into 2021, a boy young enough to be my child ushered me past the National Guard checkpoint and through the white medical tent where I verified my credentials for vaccination. I passed into a large hall ringed with hospital beds and was told to wait in line. When my time came, I walked to the nurses' station and made small talk as a sweet, charming woman old enough to be my grandmother inoculated me against the plague. I wept tears of joy and sadness. Joy for the capacity of the human heart — to strive, to fight and not to yield. Sadness for the lies and denial that led to so many needless deaths.

Weeks later, as my boys sat dead-eyed in the pharmacy's backroom absorbing the prick of the vaccine's needle, my tears flowed freely once more. Maybe we could start living again.

YEARS have passed now since we traveled to California. With each passing week the earth grows angrier with heat and fires and once-in-a-lifetime storms. Whether due to Coronavirus or the climate, if we had waited a year, there would have been no way we could have made the same trip.

When COVID first came and the deaths mounted and the world began to shut down, I felt strongly sustained by our time away. The Road. The Surf. The Desert. The Canyon. The Valley. The Mountains. The Trees. When so much was unknown and the nagging sense of fear made me feel as empty as a picked over grocery store shelf, these were my constant companions.

On my knees each night I prayed we would see this through. I prayed for the health and safety of my wife and children. For my parents, my brother, my extended family and friends. I prayed for strangers alone in ICU beds and the families they left behind. And I prayed for our world leaders that they might be brave enough to make the hard decisions needed to lead us through this mess. But when the silence that answered those prayers was too much for me, I turned my mind back to the woods and the trail, the never-ending sky all consuming, and my spirit swelled with the truth that nothing in this human lifetime is eternal. But the spirit — the spirit is a whole different matter.

WHEN we first returned from out West, even though my eyes and heart felt newly adjusted to the wonders of the world, I was surprised to see that not much else really changed. That's when I realized, metaphors aside, that there really is no such thing as a reset button in life. You've just got to live with your mistakes, your heartbreaks, and all of the doors you weren't brave enough to open or close — all of the paths you chose not to take. You've just got to play on in the ever-changing twilight of the near and beating Now. That is all we've ever had. That is all we've ever needed.

THE other day I was driving down the thruway, the family van loaded to the gills, on the way to a campground on Cape Cod for a few days by the ocean. The initial bickering of the trip had burnt off and Theresa was slack-jawed and sleeping next to me. Henry was on his phone. Max was reading. Harper was drawing sweet pictures in her notebook with a set of miniature colored pencils she bought with her own money for the trip.

As the cars and trucks whizzed passed me, full of people on their way, I felt this great opening in my chest. I don't know if I can really describe it. It was like a cracking, a splintering without sound. Joy came rushing in. And my soul expanded outward down the road. I wasn't just *me* anymore. I was the truck driver hauling freight. The hipster tapping a beat in his Tesla. The NRA guy spewing black filth into the sky from two chrome smoke stacks. Just like a redwood, I was more than the sum of my parts. It was the weirdest thing. Call it mystical or whatever, but all at once I felt this sacred connection with everything around me. Like I was part of it in this intimate way — no, like *we* were part of it. All of us. Spokes in the wheel of the greater whole.

HENRY turns 16 this year. Soon he'll be driving. Max is set to be a teenager. He's got a razor now for the fuzz above his lip. And Harper's going to be a decade old. She's the sweetest thing in my life.

Theresa and I still hold hands some times. We walk together whenever we can. Old friends that we are, there will always be love between us.

As for me, I can't make any more promises. Life's a leaf's fall too short for that. But there is beauty to be found as we tumble. I have seen it. I am certain of that for sure.

And when the time comes for us to be together, there is only one last thing I ask. That you first think of me driving on the crust of the California coast, hand out the window in the wind, heading toward the stunning silence of the desert. And I'll come walking up the path in the canyon. You'll know it's me by the company I keep: three growing angels and a companion by my side. And I'll shine out to you over the desolate valley, we'll climb the mountains, touch the sky. Leap together into the wide-open windsong and wash our laughter in the cool waters we meet. And when the shadows finally start to grow longer and the forest swells thick and ferny under your feet, look up into the yearning branches of the ragged redwoods, for there you'll find my spirit waiting on the same wind that curls the tide. And my hand will always be open. The time for fists is over and done. All I hope is we can make it back together, taking the longest way home as we ride.

Acknowledgements

I am blessed to have many friends and early readers who gave budding drafts of this book their full attention and care — among them: Luke Gutelius, Kristen Farrell, Kayla Storto, and Kim Phillips. Ben Schafer's editorial eye was honest, tough and fair, and though I didn't always follow his advice, (sorry, Ben), I am nevertheless grateful for it. I am humbled to call fellow writers, Emily McDonnell and Richard Robison members of my storytelling family. Their respective visions of the world both inspire me and give me hope. As does the artful eye of Diane Bond and her brilliant daughter, Anna whose guidance with the design and layout of this book helped make it what it is.

Thanks to Mark Pogodinski and the other good folks at No Frills Buffalo. It's good to know there are people who still believe that every story matters.

My family and I encountered many "trip angels" both as we prepared for our journey and at various stops along the way. By loaning us gear, offering up advice, providing directions and shelter, and generally looking out for our well-being, these heroes — both named and unnamed in this book — made so much of what we experienced on the road possible. Thank you.

Most importantly, I offer up my love and gratitude to my wife and children. Each of you has so many gifts to give this world. I am humbled by your presence in my life. This story wouldn't be possible without you. Blest be the tie that binds.

www.ingramcontent.com/pod-product-compliance
Lightning Source LLC
Chambersburg PA
CBHW072210150726

48002CB00005B/1753